When the time came to find ⎯⎯⎯⎯⎯⎯ ⎯tal prayer authority in Texas, Thomas Schlueter's name was presented to me. We met in Austin and I presented him a large, golden key representing his authority in days ahead to influence this state, and consequently the nation. There is no one better to write a book like this than Thomas Schlueter. Not only does he operate in this authority, the ability to communicate the authority of a gatekeeper in his writing is incredible. A gate is a place of establishing authority. We each have gates in our life and spheres that the Lord has given us to rule over. This book will assist you in learning how to rule at your gate. Nehemiah is a wonderful picture of an administrative leader who moved to restore a broken city and establish new authority in that city. Keeper of the Keys is a transformational book that I highly recommend for every leader.

Dr. Chuck D. Pierce
President, Global Spheres Inc. President,
Glory of Zion International

Thomas Schlueter, pastor of Prince of Peace House of Prayer in Texas and statewide coordinator of the Texas Apostolic Prayer Network, understands the importance of being a gatekeeper for the Kingdom. Like a Nehemiah, he has received favor with city-wide, statewide and national leaders who oversee gates of governmental leadership. Thomas also was a key helper in making sure that my work, Well Versed, was distributed to the entire Texas Legislature as well as to Governor Abbott, Lt. Governor Patrick and Attorney General Paxton. It is definitely a season of restoration and reformation in our nation, and Keeper of the Keys brings a thorough understanding of our role and responsibility as courageous restorers of the breach. The walls are being built. The gates are being restored. You are a keeper of keys and this book will help ignite your passion for the task.

Dr. Jim Garlow
Senior Pastor of Skyline Church, San Diego

The hard but rewarding work of a city's transformation begins with our own personal journey. No man or woman has taken a city for Christ when the strongholds of a city lie within that individual. Tom and Kay Schlueter have faithfully fathered the good, decent, and godly forerunners of the faith in the highways and byways of Texas. They have labored with love in the harvest force (church) of Gods kingdom nurturing them to take Jesus to the harvest fields. Their organic ministry to Gods laborers in the work of city transformation has high value. The result will be a trademark of God left on our cities and state forever.

Randy H. Skinner
Inner City Missionary
President and Founder
Strategic Justice Initiatives Inc.
Dallas, Texas

The Church has been given principles and keys to see lives, communities (and cultural spheres), even nations impacted. Tom Schlueter, in his book reminds us that we have been entrusted as stewards of the keys that have been given by the Lord. I've personally known Pastor Tom Schlueter for many years, and have observed a consistency and passion for God and people that is not just demonstrated in words, but action. His dedication to undergird, encourage, empower, and connect many, not just in the church world, but those in all areas of leadership and government, is seen in the fruit of the significant network of leaders he serves. Prayer is not just a hobby to him, but he truly understands the power of prayer, and the strategic wisdom and insights that the Lord reveals as a result of that intimate place of communication with the One who holds all the Keys.

Doug Stringer
Somebody Cares America

This is a day when God is speaking to His people, as never before, about transforming our cities. The number one biblical example of city transformation is the rebuilding of Jerusalem. In Keeper of the Keys, Tom

Schlueter skillfully draws out and analyzes the principles from the story and gives us practical directives for applying them today.

Dr. C. Peter Wagner
Presiding Apostle, Global Spheres Inc.

*The God of Heaven will prosper us; therefore, we His servants will arise and build*

- NEHEMIAH 2:20

Build... that is the season we are in. Tom Schlueter has provided an amazing blueprint to follow in order to unlock the Kingdom and build. His insight provides the understanding needed to "work with one hand and hold a weapon in the other. The anointing "to finish" is on every page. Read and Finish Well.

Apostle Sandy Newman
Destiny Ministries
Arkansas City, Kansas

# KEEPER OF THE KEYS

# KEEPER OF THE KEYS

When the People of God are Ignited to Produce Cultural Transformation

Dr Thomas R Schlueter

ISBN-13: 9781973906629
ISBN-10: 1973906627

# Dedication

*To the true Keeper of the Keys – Jesus Christ.*
*You named me as a Keeper of the Keys.*
*"For this reason, I bow my knees to the Father of our*
*Lord Jesus Christ, from whom the whole family in heaven*
*and earth is named" (Ephesians 3:14, 15).*

*For Prince of Peace Church*
*A Key to Unlock the Heavenlies*

*As I was writing this book, the Lord continued to impress upon me that I was merely a scribe that was writing the testimony of the congregation I serve. In March of 2009, I was gathering soil from our ground around the church. It was to be sent to Oklahoma to be blessed by Dr. Negiel Bigpond and Dr. Jay Swallow of the Two Rivers Native American Training Center. They asked that the name and location of the dirt be placed on the bag as well as a one-line description of the place where the dirt was located. As I wrote on the bag the Lord declared: "Prince of Peace Church is a key that will unlock the treasures of heaven." Even on our website an overhead picture of our building shows a key-shaped structure.*

*The members and friends of this congregation are the ones, individually and corporately that will open the door and invite the King of Glory to come in. This book is dedicated to the faithful priests and intercessors of this congregation who have taken up the call to be a kingdom of priests and who truly invite the Lord to reign over their lives and the life of the city, the State of Texas and the nation. This book is ultimately their story – their testimony – which is being released. I personally thank them for their faith, their prayers, their gifts and their support which have allowed the possibility of this book.*

# Acknowledgments

My deep thanks…

To my wife, Kay, and my family (Josh, Andrea, Nate, Luke, Tim, Katie, TJ, Anna, Allan and Amy) who encourage and strengthen me with their constant love. I love you.

To Apostle John Benefiel for his servant heart which has caused me to excel.

To Apostle Jay Swallow who has imparted a deep love for the land which God so desperately desires to heal and restore. I miss you!

To Apostle Dutch Sheets who has demonstrated to me the authority of our decrees and intercessions.

To Apostle and Prophet Chuck Pierce who declared to me "I've got your back" as I was set into place as the apostolic coordinator of the Texas Apostolic Prayer Network.

To David Munoz for his beautiful cover artwork

To my friends and co-laborers in Arlington, Texas and throughout all of the states of Texas, Oklahoma, Louisiana, New Mexico, Kansas, Arkansas and the heartland of America. We will see the Lord come into our midst. We will witness His kingdom come!

To Jeanine Smith who edited the work with me – covering it with prayer.

To Renee Hughen who applied the principles of the book through her prayer network in the Anglican Church of Arkansas.

And once again, to the members of Prince of Peace Church, who make pastoring a profound joy. Thank you for your love. Thank you for your support. Thank you for embracing the true intent that God has for your lives.

To Mom and Dad, who love me, encourage me, and pray for me.

# Table of Contents

# Foreword

As I journey through this temporal life trying to make an eternal impact, the answers to three questions have become all important factors for me. They should be for all of us. In fact, if you don't have accurate answers to all three, you will never be completely successful at attaining your destiny and being a difference-maker on the earth. For some, that won't matter – most people don't have ambitions of making things better in the world. Simply being prosperous and happy is their idea of fulfillment. But if you've picked up a book on this subject, you're probably the kind of person that would like to make a difference in the affairs of mankind.

Concerning these three questions, I'm pleased to inform you that Tom Schlueter's book on Nehemiah, Keeper of the Keys, addresses all of them in a most insightful way. I expect no less from Tom, considering the blend of intelligence, revelation, wisdom and practicality with which God has gifted him. Nevertheless, though expected, the depth with which he addresses them is refreshing and revelatory. As you read his well-reasoned thoughts and divinely inspired enlightenment, I'm sure you'll agree.

The first question that must be answered in every situation and every season is simply, "what is God doing?" Ecclesiastes makes clear the fact that there are seasons and timings for every event, and that everything is "appropriate" in its time (see Ecclesiastes 3:1-11). One of the keys to success, therefore, is to uncover God's timing. As Tom has observed, the story of Nehemiah demonstrates this and points out that it will always involve God's heart of restoring that which sin and Satan have damaged or destroyed. He is a redemptive God! Tom makes the point that God's restoration, which is His kingdom coming to our world, moves us from chaos to order and from death to life. When the early church in Acts was accused by unbelievers of turning their world "upside down," it is fitting that the Greek word translated as such literally means, "to stand upright." The world's upside down is often God's right side up! Find out what God wants done, begin to do it, and you have stepped into the realm of His favor.

Keeper of the Keys also highlights the importance of understanding our opposition. "What is Satan doing?" has become a question I ask myself regularly. We don't have to be preoccupied with our enemy to be aware of his tactics and plans. Some teach that we should ignore the devil, saying, "Christ has already dealt with him." Scripture, however, admonishes us to not be ignorant of Satan's devices or schemes so that he won't take advantage of us (see 2 Corinthians 2:11). Daniel tells us that one of the ways Satan tries to defeat us is to hinder God's plans and timing (see Daniel 7:25). Knowing how he does this enables us to keep it from happening. Tom gives wise counsel on discerning these schemes of the enemy – invaluable insights if we're to see our world righted.

But there is one more question we must answer if we are going to see God's kingdom come and His will be done in our lives and world: "what is my part?" As Tom so aptly points out, we are the "gates" through whom God desires to enter our world. While we often look for the right method, God looks for the right person. People are God's methods! "I sought for a man" (see Ezekiel 22:30-31) is always God's plan for the entrance of His kingdom into earthly chaos. Turning the world right side up is not just the work of God and angels – it is the work of Spirit-led and Spirit-empowered people. Discovering our realm of influence and fulfilling our God-given role therein, should be a lifelong pursuit as we partner with God in restoring His will in the earth. We should never settle for less. Keeper of the Keys makes this truth clear in a powerful way.

You are holding in your hands a true manual for transformation. Read it and apply its timeless truths. If you do, you will move from the mundane cares of life and the status quo dreams of so many, into God's exciting world of healing the hurting, restoring the broken, and life-ing the lifeless. Join the revolution!

**Apostle Dutch Sheets**
Dutch Sheets Ministries
Colorado Springs, Colorado

# A Special Second Edition Introduction

April 14, 2017
Global Spheres Center – Corinth, Texas

I saw one who was carrying out his normal duties as a loyal worker or servant. All of a sudden, a shift took place in the atmosphere. A change was coming. A servant becomes a leader. A cupbearer becomes a builder.

Last summer in 2016, the Lord strongly impressed upon me, during prayer, that He was bringing His people, His church, out of Babylon. I've been praying for that season to come forth. Not long after that revelation, Lance Wallnau begin to speak of Donald J. Trump being as a Cyrus according to Isaiah 45.

As we came into the first month of the year in Nissan 2017 (5777), the Lord strongly impressed upon me that it is time now for Nehemiah to be noticed by King Artaxerxes. The Lord informed that even though I had written this book years prior, now was the season of Nehemiah. During the month of Nissan, Nehemiah, a cupbearer before the king, is seen by the king as one who has sorrow on his face. As the king asked him why the sorrow, Nehemiah proclaims how could I not be sorrowful when the walls and the gates of my city are still down.

Artaxerxes commissions Nehemiah to go back to Jerusalem and to rebuild the gates and the walls of his city. And it wasn't a suggestion or instruction, but a royal decree for him to go back. And not only a decree to build, but also Artaxerxes makes all the provision necessary. Artaxerxes gave him permission, provision and protection to go and build. Now is the time for Nehemiah to be once again sent out. He is to make ready the walls and the gates again for the kingdom. And the Lord will make sure that all the provision that is needed will be granted on to the people.

At that Global Spheres Center at Passover 2017 (5777), I heard the Lord say, "Now is the time to move into the destiny. Pass over. I saw one who was carrying out his normal duties as a loyal worker or servant. All of a sudden, a shift took place in the atmosphere. A change was coming. A servant becomes a leader. A cupbearer becomes a builder."

This was similar to a visitation I had with the Lord in October 2016 as I travelled home from Washington DC. He invited me to walk up steps, with Him, into a new realm of anointing and authority. He robed not only me but all of us with a diamond-like armor and lifted us up into a swirling whirlwind of angelic activity. Passover now!

The gates and walls of Jerusalem were finished in 52 days on the 25th of Elul. Although the month of Elul — the sixth month of the Jewish year, which immediately precedes Rosh Hashanah — has no special importance in the Bible or in early rabbinic writings, various customs arose sometime during the first millennium that designated Elul as the time to prepare for the High Holy Days. Not only is Elul a precursor to Rosh Hashanah, but October 2017 is also the 500th anniversary of the Reformation. Because these days are filled with so much meaning and potency, they require a special measure of readiness. Fifty-two days prior to this date, which is September 16 (eve of the 15th) on our calendar, is the 4th of Av (July 27, 2017 on our calendar). It is a season for Nehemiah. But these months will also bring about great trial as Sanballat, Tobiah and Geshem will pour out their greatest obstacles to stop the work, BUT GOD…

It is interesting and exciting to know that on the morning of his inauguration as our 45th president, Donald Trump attended a prayer service. Dr. Robert Jeffress of First Baptist Church in Dallas gave the message. Here is that message:

### When God Chooses a Leader

NEHEMIAH 1:11

*Introduction: President-elect and Mrs. Trump, Vice-President-elect and Mrs. Pence, families and friends, it's an honor to be with you on this historic day. President-elect Trump, I remember that it was exactly one year ago this weekend that I was with you on your Citation jet flying around Iowa before the first caucus or primary vote was cast. After our Wendy's cheeseburgers, I said that I believed that you would be the next President of the United States. And if that happened, it would be because God had placed you there. As the prophet Daniel said, it is God who removes and establishes leaders.*

*Today – one year later – God has raised you and Vice-President-elect Pence up for a great, eternal purpose. When I think of you, President-elect Trump, I am reminded of another great leader God chose thousands of years ago in Israel. The nation had been in bondage for decades, the infrastructure of the country was in shambles, and God raised up a powerful leader to restore the nation. And the man God chose was neither a politician nor a priest. Instead, God chose a builder whose name was Nehemiah.*

*And the first step of rebuilding the nation was the building of a great wall. God instructed Nehemiah to build a wall around Jerusalem to protect its citizens from enemy attack. You see, God is NOT against building walls! And the Old Testament book of Nehemiah records how Nehemiah completed that massive project in record time – just 52 days. Why was Nehemiah so successful in building the wall and rebuilding the nation?*

**I. Nehemiah Refused to Allow His Critics to Distract Him**

*Someone has said there are three guaranteed ways to avoid criticism: do nothing, say nothing, and be nothing. Any true leader is going to face criticism. President-elect Trump, you have had your share of critics from the day you announced you were running for President, but you've confounded them at every turn. First, they said you couldn't win the nomination, but you ended up garnering the most votes of any Republican in history. Then they said that was a fluke, but you couldn't win the election. And you handily* defeated your opponent. And now your critics say you can't possibly succeed in your agenda.

Nehemiah had his own share of critics. Two of his chief antagonists were named Sanballat and Tobiah. They were the mainstream media of their day. They continued to hound and heckle Nehemiah and spread false rumors while he and the Israelites were building the wall. At one point, they said, "Nehemiah, you need to stop the project and come down from the wall and have a meeting with us."

Nehemiah's response was classic: "I'm doing a great work . . . why should I stop the work and come down to you?" (Nehemiah 6:3) President-elect Trump, you, Vice President-elect Pence, and your team have been called by God and elected by the people to do a great work. It is a work far too important to stop and answer your critics.

## II. Nehemiah Refused to Allow Setbacks to Stop Him

As you read through Nehemiah's journal, you'll find that he faced tremendous obstacles as he attempted to rebuild the nation: an economic recession, terrorist attacks from enemies, and discouragement among the citizens. But none of those setbacks was enough to stop Nehemiah. Some years ago, two sports commentators on television were discussing the late Hall of Famer Walter Peyton, the running back for the Chicago Bears. One commentator said, "Can you believe that during his career Peyton has run more than nine miles with a football?"

The other commentator replied, "What's even more amazing is that every 3.8 yards of those nine miles Peyton got knocked down by a guy twice his size! But he got back up every time and kept moving forward in spite of those bruising hits and hard knocks."

President Trump, you, your team and your families are going to face some bruising setbacks. But remember. The true measure of a leader is what it takes to stop him. And knowing you, I believe it's going to take a lot to stop you.

## III. Nehemiah Sought God's Help to Empower Him

Nehemiah was a gifted leader, but he knew he could not succeed without God's divine help. And that is why as he began the great work, Nehemiah knelt before God and prayed: "O Lord, let your ear be attentive to the prayer of this your servant who delights in revering your name. Give your servant success today . . ." (Nehemiah 1:11)

Mr. President-elect, I don't believe we have ever had a president with as many natural gifts as you. As you know, the reason I endorsed you within weeks of your announcement that you were running was because I believed that you were the only candidate who possessed the leadership skills necessary to reverse the downward trajectory of our nation. And beginning with Vice President-elect Pence – a great and godly man – you've assembled an unbelievably talented group of advisers around you. But the challenges facing our nation are so great that it will take more than natural ability to meet them. We need God's supernatural power.

The good news is that the same God who empowered Nehemiah nearly 2500 years ago is available to every one of us today who is willing to humble himself and ask for His help. God says in Psalm 50:15 "Call upon Me in the day of trouble I shall rescue you and you will honor Me."

When President Ronald Reagan addressed the Republican National Convention in my city of Dallas in 1984 he said, "America needs God more than God needs America. If we ever forget that we are "one nation under God," then we will be a nation gone under."

President-elect Trump, you had a campaign slogan that resonated with tens of millions of Americans because it spoke to their heartfelt desire: "Make America Great Again." Psalm 33:12 gives us the starting point for making that happen: "Blessed – great – is the nation whose God is the Lord."

May God bless President-elect Trump, Vice-President-elect Pence, their families and advisers. And may God truly bless the United States of America.


"But you are a chosen race, a royal priesthood, a holy nation, a people for his own possession, that you may proclaim the excellencies of him who called you out of darkness into his marvelous light. Once you were not a people, but now you are God's people; once you had not received mercy, but now you have received mercy" (1 Peter 2:9-10 ESV).

Dr. Thomas Schlueter

# Introduction

> *"So, I became dreadfully afraid, and said to the king, 'May the king live forever! Why should my face not be sad, when the city, the place of my fathers' tombs, lies waste, and its gates are burned with fire?'"*

> *(NEHEMIAH 2:2B,3).*

On Sunday morning, October 28, 2004, I saw and heard the following vision:

The Lord walked with me to Mt. Scopus, which overlooks the city of Jerusalem. We overlooked the city, but I questioned in my heart, "Why are we here, Lord? Let's go to where it is quiet."

And He said, "Tom, this is My city. It is My heart."

We walked the city streets. They were old. They were dilapidated. They were broken down, but they were filled with people.

I noticed very clearly in the vision that Jesus was hugging the people. He was stopping and ministering to everyone. He played with the children. He smiled. He was beaming with delight with the people. He chuckled when He saw a man struggling to get his donkey to move, and He went and helped him.

Jesus said, "Tom, I love this city. I love the people. I died for them. I died for you. Love your city, Tom. Walk it. Pray for it. Give your all to it."

When He began to speak that, I had some fear coming over me. My first impression was, "Lord, I don't really know if I want to die for the city."

"He said, "Don't fear. I see your fears. You don't have to die for them. I've done that. But, I do want you to give yourself over to them in My name. Continue to love them as you drive, as you shop, do not despise any."

I started thinking of other things, and I realized the Lord had moved on ahead of me. I called out to Him, and He said, "Come stay with Me. Don't lag behind. Don't fret. Don't try to figure this out. Just come to Me. Take My hand. Let's walk on."

As soon as I did, everything became dark. Everything became dark. Pitch dark. I couldn't see anything. "Lord, what is this?"

His answer to me was, "This is the heart of the church."

I said, "What do You mean?"

He said, "They have become darkened. Many of them are no longer seeing Me."

"What am I to do?"

He gave me no answer.

We walked on. It became darker and darker if it could possibly become darker. Then I saw a ray of light. It was like a gem or diamond with an iridescent glow – a very light iridescent glow just hanging out there. I couldn't really see anything around it except that the Lord was holding it.

I said, "What is this, Lord?"

And He said, "This is My heart. I want you to take it."

As I took it into my hands, I felt warmth and light coursing through me and over me. And I said, "Lord, Your love – It is overwhelming!"

Then light began to be released to everything around me. Now I was seeing the city again, but now the city was completely restored. It had new streets, new buildings – The buildings were all polished and beautiful. I knew that it wasn't Heaven. It literally was the city. Whether it was the City of Jerusalem or not, I cannot say, but I do know that it was a restored city, and everything about it was beautiful.

The Lord finished by saying, "Embrace Me, Tom, and help them to embrace Me. Pray for them. Build the walls anew, Nehemiah." I literally heard Him call me "Nehemiah." So, at that point I knew that I had to begin to do a study of Nehemiah to see what the Lord is saying through this book that we need to hear.

As you will discover in the coming chapters, the book of Nehemiah is filled with images of walls and gates. The Lord revealed to me His desire for each of us to understand the importance of these images. When I asked for further clarification regarding Nehemiah the Lord informed me that He desires to release the fullness of His kingdom into this earth and He needs gates to accomplish the task.

My wife, Kay and I enjoyed watching the television series entitled Stargate SG-1. The premise of this sci-fi adventure is centered on the use of ancient gates that will transport a team (SG-1) from earth to another planet or galaxy in as matter of seconds through the use of a wormhole. After the team arrives they usually face some evil force or person that desires to dominate the inhabitants of the local planet and destroy their freedom to live. Interestingly the names of these evil forces are ancient names like Baal, Anubis and Ra.

I am not recommending that you run out and rent the series, but I do want to make it clear that the Lord desires the same thing. The main exception is this – He desires to enter into our world in order that it can be taken back as His kingdom. Evil forces need to be destroyed. Transformation needs to take place. Lives need to be liberated by His grace and power to save. And the Lord needs gates to accomplish the task.

Another strong impression the Lord gave me was that gates are not only represented by what we see as physical gates, doors or entryways. Our understanding of gates needs to be infused with the wisdom and revelation of God. For instance, rivers can be gates. A gate can be a remote piece of ground out in the middle of nowhere. Highways in and out of a city or state are gates. And most importantly – in the pages to follow we will discover that people are gates. And people are not only gates but are gatekeepers. **They are the keepers of the keys.** The Lord began to reveal to me through my opening vision and my subsequent studies of Nehemiah that all these gates will be used by Him to bring forth His kingdom into this world.

The book of Nehemiah has been very instrumental to me throughout the years of my ministry. I first preached on Nehemiah about eighteen months after I came as pastor to Prince of Peace Church in 1988. Portions of that sermon are still vividly embedded in my memory. The message of Nehemiah contains a key element in understanding and releasing God's kingdom into the earth. It is instrumental in answering the prayer, "Your kingdom come and Your will be done on earth as it is in heaven."

Over the course of this book, I will share some dreams, visions, words from the Lord, experiences and events that will give us a feel about why the Lord is releasing this into our hearts. I also want what I write to be very practical. This message is not my own, but a revelation that Lord is making to His church in this hour. The Lord has placed each of us in key positions as gates in order to release His kingdom into our world through intercession and declaration.

In my book, Return of the Priests, God showed me that intercession is not a special gift or anointing. Intercession is a position. God desires that we intercede or pray for others in whatever place or position He has appointed for us. A woman, in her position as mother, will pray for her children. A man, in his position as father, will pray for his family. An individual, in the position of employer, will pray for those who work at his or her company. People, in their position as citizens, will intercede for their city or nation. God showed me that Jesus was in the perfect position of intercession as He hung upon the cross. Jesus prayed from the cross, but it was not His prayers that saved us. It was His position of intercession between God and our sins that saved us from the judgment we deserve.[1] The position He is putting each of us in during this kairos moment in history is as gates! God wants each of us to step into our divinely appointed position in order to release His redemptive restoration of our hearts, homes, congregations, cities, states and nation.

LET US PRAY.

Lord, I am asking that You would release into each heart, into each life a fuller awareness of the intimacy we have in You. Lord, I'm asking one thing very specifically. You showed me Your heart as an iridescent glowing diamond or gem. Lord, would You place that in every reader's heart right now? Would you release it to them so that they would come fully and completely into an intimate and tender relationship with You? Only then can we can do what You've called us to do as Your redeemed people. We are to be instruments of Your redemptive purpose so that we can see the city, the state, the nation and the nations come into alignment – whether it be Arlington or Burma, whether it be Papua New Guinea or China, whether it be Honduras or our workplace on Monday morning. Lord, we thank You that You have given us the authority and that we will move in that authority to see the restoration of all that is around us to the glory of Jesus Christ. We lift up our heads as gates and invite the King of Glory to come in! In His name we pray, Amen.

# The Season of Nehemiah

*"The words of Nehemiah the son of Hachaliah: It came to pass in the month of Chislev, in the twentieth year, as I was in Shushan the citadel…"*

*(NEHEMIAH 1:1-2B).*

In late spring of 2007 I attended a "Light the Highway" organizational meeting hosted by Cindy Jacobs. "Light the Highway" is a worldwide movement to bring reformation to cities, regions and entire nations as thousands of believers commit themselves to personal and corporate holiness along their "highway".[2] It primarily focused on Interstate 35 that runs north and south in the heart of the United States. It took root following prophetic words by Cindy Jacobs and Sam Brassfield.

At this gathering, I met Sam Brassfield for the first time. Cindy introduced him to me. He immediately proceeded in sharing a portion of a word that the Lord had given him regarding the year 2008. He was unaware of my study of Nehemiah and gates. He declared to me that in January of 2007 he was awakened by the Holy Spirit. The Spirit declared to him: "2008 will be the year of the **GATES!**"[3]

His word stunned and excited me. The Lord had given me revelation at a key time. Sam's words point out the importance of God's seasons and timings regarding gates.

Even as I am finishing the last edit of this manuscript we have entered into the Hebrew year of 5768 which is called Samekh Chet. The Hebrew number "eight" is the Chet. It looks like a gate. It is a year of new beginnings. It is year of the gate. In the time since I saw the vision I recorded in the Introduction, the Lord has been granting me one confirmation after another that this is indeed a "Season of Nehemiah." And as I revise the first edition of this book, we are only months away from 5778. At Rosh Hashanah 2017 (5778) we will enter another Chet (gate) year. The most significant confirmation I discovered was in the first verse of Nehemiah.

"The words of Nehemiah the son of Hachaliah: It came to pass in the month of Chislev, in the twentieth year, as I was in Shushan the citadel..." (Nehemiah 1:1-2b).

The first thing the Lord revealed to me was that the message of Nehemiah is a message for now! There is something that He wants to stir in our lives, cities, state and nation right now that is significant. The Hebrew month of Chislev corresponds to our months of November and December. So, when the Lord began to speak to me during November and December of 2004 about the "Season of Nehemiah" I realized that I was not supposed to hesitate in asking Him to open my eyes to His revelations regarding the book. I was to begin looking right then during the 11th and 12th months of the year at the book of Nehemiah. And I did. The Lord began the process of further revelation as we obediently meditated on Nehemiah in the latter part of 2004.

Significance of the Numbers

Another thing that is significant about this timing is that in the Hebrew symbolism of numbers, the numbers "eleven" and "twelve" are very important. The number "eleven" is considered an incomplete number. It is also a number that signifies "transition." The complete numbers in the Hebrew system are always based on seven, on ten or on twelve or on the multiples thereof. So, when you look at "seventy times seven", for instance, when Jesus is referring to forgiveness or when you are talking about the "twelve" Apostles or the "seven" Days of Creation, the "seven" Last Words of Christ, the "seven" churches in Revelation – all of these words are saying that everything is complete. Everything is put together in its right place.[4]

But on the other hand, "eleven" is incomplete. The totally incomplete numbers are multiples of any of those numbers. Even though the number is far more significant than this, I believe that the number 666, the symbolic number for the Antichrist, is totally anti-anything that is God – totally out of order – totally chaotic – totally dark – totally incomplete. Anything that falls short of the perfect numbers is a totally incomplete number. The number "eleven" in the Hebrew symbolism stands for incompleteness, disorganization, disintegration, lawlessness, disorder and can also refer to the antichrist.[5]

That sense of incompletion is what I was feeling when I began to see the city in that vision. I saw the city dilapidated. I saw it broken down. I saw it incomplete. I did see God's mercy flowing into it through Jesus, but it was incomplete. Interestingly, as soon as I left that portion of the vision, I went into darkness. So, the whole number "eleven" was very significant to me in the sense that we are living in an incomplete age. We are living in things that are not put completely into order yet. We just have to look at things around us, and we see things incomplete and out of order, in darkness.

## DARKNESS CAN BE GOOD

"So, the people stood afar off, but Moses drew near the thick darkness where God was" (Exodus 20:21).

Moses drew near the thick darkness where God was. I do not believe that all the darkness in this dream meant evil and confusion. The darkness had a positive aspect in that it made me feel vulnerable and helpless. It was "pitch dark." In reviewing my feelings in the midst of the vision – I felt humbled, useless and insignificant. But in the midst of that darkness the Lord approached me and mantled me with His light and strength. George Otis, Jr. of The Sentinel Group was speaking at an event held by the Greater Dallas Prayer Ministry. He declared that God is in the darkness and that He draws us into that place so that we realize that the work of the kingdom and transformation does not happen via our strength, our strategies or our wisdom. In the darkness those vanish and we must embrace our only hope – Jesus the Light.[6]

## THE NUMBER TWELVE

Just as "eleven" is an incomplete number, the number "twelve" is a complete number. It signifies the number of divine government. More specifically, "twelve" speaks of apostolic fullness.[7] It means that everything is going to come into all that it was intended to be. Everything is going to come into its apostolic fullness. And the true apostle is Jesus Christ. Everything is going to come into fullness in Jesus Christ.

So, as we study the numbers "eleven" and "twelve," we should see a progression or transition from disintegration and chaos into order and alignment. We are not destined to stay in chaos until Jesus comes and sets everything into fullness and order. Even though we will witness the complete perfection of all things when He returns, God is saying, "I want to begin to restore things NOW."

Please don't misunderstand me. I'm not saying that on this side of heaven we are going to progressively get perfect. I am saying that we are progressing in our relationship with Jesus to the point that we are overcomers. We are being raised up as an Army of God. We are being raised up as those who would pursue and take possession of that which has been promised to us. We are being fashioned as gates to allow God's light, order, transformation and glory to enter into this earth realm. As I shared in my book, Return of the Priests, we are moving into a season where we return to the dominion intended for us in the Garden. As saints and priests of God after the order of Melchizedek, we are seeking for "His Kingdom (to) come and His will (to be) done on earth as it is in heaven" (Matthew 6:10, emphasis mine).

## A SHORT VISIT WITH ADAM AND MELCHIZEDEK

I mentioned that we need to return to the dominion intended for us in the garden. Adam and Eve were given the privilege to be the first priests, and in the context of this book – the first gatekeepers. God granted them the privilege and responsibility of living in an intimate Spirit to spirit relationship with their Maker. Out of that relationship they would release His authority, light, love and dominion over all the earth. Adam and Eve failed at their tasks as gatekeepers. They were to live and move as royal priests, but they exchanged a life driven by the Spirit of God with a life driven by their own understanding of good and evil.

Jesus restored that which was lost. He restored our identity as royal priests.

"But you are a chosen generation, a royal priesthood, a holy nation, His own special people, that you may proclaim the praises of Him who called you out of darkness into His marvelous light; who once were not a people but are now the people of God, who had not obtained mercy but now have obtained mercy" (1 Peter 2:9-10).

Jesus is a Priest forever after the order of Melchizedek. Take joy in the fact that He is the Son of God and that He is eternal. His assignment is eternal. Jesus is eternally interceding for you. He is a Priest forever according to the order of Melchizedek.

And since Jesus Christ is after the order of Melchizedek and since we are in Christ and He is in us, we too, are after the order of Melchizedek. We are a kingdom of priests that God is raising up for this day. We are restored as gatekeepers.

## DISORDER TO ORDER

All of these things are significant as we move from eleven to twelve and as we move from disorder to order. The Lord wants to bring the Holy City of God into completion. I believe that is what the vision was about. In the end, I saw a city that was bright and beautiful and renewed and refreshed and full of light and life.

As further confirmation of this new understanding, God spoke a similar truth through Dutch Sheets the week before I preached this sermon to the congregation. I was with Beth Alves in the Intercessors International[8] board meeting. Pastor Dutch Sheets is also on the board. Dutch shared with the Board how he had traveled to all fifty states with Chuck Pierce, a prophetic voice in our time. At the end of this tour of states, a prophet had declared to Dutch, "The Lord is going to take you now to a different level. You are going to look up into the heavens and see the numbers eleven and twelve before you." Dutch said to us, "I'm not really sure what that means yet." [9]

My heart began to beat faster as he said the numbers eleven and twelve. I realized that they represented the transition from chaos to order, from disintegration into alignment and fullness. After the meeting, I said to Dutch, "I truly believe that that is going to be happening. The Lord is going to take you into some very significant places where you are going to be able to administer God's order in places that are disorderly." I also shared, "I think it has to do with right now. Don't wait until January or April or August of next year to step into what God is showing you to do." Then I showed him this revelation out of Nehemiah, and he received it. He said, "I believe you're right. This is the time that this transition is going to start being made." [10]

In his book Authority in Prayer, Dutch shares his thoughts on this transition: "Through these two numbers I felt God was saying to me, 'You must go through the disorder (11) in the heavens and exercise My kingdom authority or rule (12).' As you can imagine, with so much confirmation and orchestration by the Spirit, I fulfilled this assignment with great confidence, knowing I was obeying God's direction and moving in His authority."[11]

### From Disorder to Order – from Chaos to Apostolic Fullness

Let me summarize this issue of timing. With all my heart, I believe that we in a season when we are going to see things moving out of disorder into order. We are going to witness God bringing restoration, renewal, strengthening, brightening, a lightening, and an aligning of the cities and nations of the earth. He is a transforming God. He is bringing a person, a city or a nation into the destiny that He had intended for it.

I need to state here an important point again – transformation does not equal perfection. For instance, when God begins to transform or renew a city, what that basically means is that the city's life and destiny is now more determined by what God is doing than what Satan is doing. The city has been transformed into a place that is declaring God as its center. We have seen testimony of this through the Transformation Videos produced by George Otis and The Sentinel Group. As powerful as God is moving in those places, none of them are perfect. They are still going through sin issues. They still have problems, but they are now depending on God to be their answer rather than on man being their answer.

## LET US PRAY

Lord, we embrace Your season and calling to be gates. We deliberately move from eleven to twelve. We deliberately move from chaos to order and from darkness to light. We decide today, not tomorrow, to take up our mantle of intimate authority – as royal priests – and open up the gates to allow Your kingdom and Your will to be released into our world. To You be all the glory. Amen.

# 2

# The City and the Church

*"Is it possible, Lord, that You have a city set aside as a priest-hood? Not just the CHURCH of Arlington but the CITY of Arlington to be a redeemed city? Cannot the city be a priest - redeemed by You? Let it be, Lord, that we as a city could be a priesthood -- not just for us, but for all the cities."* [12]

## FROM THE CITY -- TO THE CHURCH -- TO THE CITY AGAIN

A significant portion of my vision was the transition that was taking place from the city to the church and back. That really puzzled me. I clearly knew that I was walking through the city of Jerusalem in the beginning part of the vision. Then as it darkened I asked the Lord, "What is this?" and He said, "It is My church." That didn't seem to fit into the vision. I thought, "Lord, wait a minute. If You are talking about Your city, let's talk about the city. If You are going to talk about the church, let's talk about the church."

The vision progressed into a revelation regarding the church. Then it went back to the city again.

I said, "Lord, I don't understand this. Would You show me what You are trying to do?" And He began to draw my thoughts to a series of revelations and experiences that He had given me in the past.

The first revelation that I will mention is in the epilogue of my book Return of the Priests. This is a record of something that took place in the sanctuary of Prince of Peace Church of Arlington, Texas in August of 2000.

### The City is a Priest

On Sunday, August 13, 2000, our congregation was gathered for an evening of intercession and worship. In the midst of our worship, the Lord began to ask me questions. He first asked...

"Tom, do you understand that you are a priest before Me?"

I answered, "Yes, Lord."

He asked again. "Tom, do you understand that every member of this congregation stands before Me as a priest?"

I answered, "Yes, Lord."

The Lord asked again, "Tom, do you understand that every saint and congregation in this city stands before Me as a priest?"

I again answered, "Yes, Lord, I do."

The Lord than asked one more question, "Tom, do you understand that I desire this whole city to stand before me as a priest?"

At that point, I began to speak prophetically to those gathered.

"Is it possible, Lord, that You have a city set aside as a priesthood?

Not just the CHURCH of Arlington - -

the CITY of Arlington

to be a redeemed city?

Cannot the city be a priest - redeemed by You?

Let it be, Lord, that we as a city could be a priesthood --

Not just for us, but for all the cities.

Take them as Your possession, Lord.

We don't know what this looks like, Lord.

Your righteousness covers the city.

Forgive me, Lord!

I had envisioned a person as a priest.

More and more You are showing me a CITY!

Your agenda, O God, is to draw <u>all</u> people unto Yourself.
Show us.

Show us, Lord.

Show us how a city can be a priesthood."[13]

That just amazes me when I think about that. That is not an image that we would normally see. We think of the Redeemed as the saints. We think of the Redeemed as the churches, the congregations. We don't normally think of the Redeemed as being the city itself. Yet, the Lord wants the city as the priest.

I still don't fully understand how He is going to bring that about, but I'm beginning to understand that we are on the right track because of the vision He gave me and also things that were being shown to me as I received the vision that is detailed in the introduction of this book.

### The People Are the Church

As I will share with you in more detail later, gates are a point of transition. Another revelation God gave me regarding this transition from city to church and then back to city should be obvious. When God transforms a city into a priesthood, the transformation will flow from the church – not the darkened religious structures I saw in the vision – but from the people or the priests/gates who have embraced the light I saw – the heart of God.

Remember in the vision, when I asked Him what He meant, God said, "This is the church. It is darkened. They are no longer seeing Me." When He showed me the light, He said, "Hold on to it because that light represents My heart."

And when I took hold of His heart, everything came to light.

What came to light was the CITY!

I truly believe that each of us as we embrace the Lord

as we seek His face

as we grab a hold of His heart

as we take a hold of that which is intimate in Him,

He will release to us that which will transform the city.

I could phrase it this way –

THE CITY WILL NEVER BE CHANGED BY THE RELIGIOUS STRUCTURE OF THE CHURCH.

Never in history has the church been changed by religious structure. Transformation is never going to happen that way. Transformation is not going to happen just because someone comes across the right formula, strategy or event. Transformation is not going to happen because one of the congregations in a city of 300,000 gets up to 100,000 members. And transformation is not going to happen when 100 churches all get together and do the same thing. Religious structures can be full of energy and amazing vision, but that is no guarantee that City Hall has been redeemed or that God's Spirit is moving through the schools or that the life of the city is more in tune with God then with Satan or man.

A city is transformed by the heart of people who have caught a passion for God and as gates open up the city to the King of Glory. Always! The Lord is saying, "I'm going to move the rehabilitation of the city through the heart of the church." The church is not a building – but the people who have a redeemed and intimate relationship with Jesus. That's you, folks. When the people within the city who have caught the heart of God release the authority God has placed in them, I believe transformation will come about. God has given us the keys to open these doors to transformation. As I mentioned earlier these words can be synonymous but we are keepers of keys which will as gatekeepers open the gates to the King and His kingdom.

Signs of the Times

In May 2002, I led a work of intercession where we had over one hundred intercessors from twenty-five different church in the city of Arlington walk the forty-four miles around the city. We did it seven times over a seven-week period. On my second leg of the trip my team was walking along a section of western Arlington. We were very near a portion of land that had witnessed a Native American massacre at the hands of the Texas Militia in 1841. As I walked and prayed I heard the cries of women and children. I turned my head only to see a large empty field, but I was clearly hearing their cries. Through that experience I discovered that gates were not just physical or natural doors. They were defined by significant "locations" where either righteousness or unrighteousness had gained access into our world.

In closing out this chapter, I'd like to share some of the experiences or events I have witnessed that I believe have been signs of God's desire to transform the city, the region or the nation. God is taking us from chaos into His order.

### Bird's Fort/Village Creek

On May 25, 2004, in response to my experience of hearing the cries of Native American women and children, I gathered pastors, prayer leaders and intercessors from the Dallas-Fort Worth region for a strategic meeting with Dr. John Benefiel (Oklahoma Apostolic Prayer Network leader) and Dr. Jay Swallow (Native American Apostle to the Native American Tribes in the United States). We dealt with issues regarding Bird's Fort and Village Creek. There were over 30 people in attendance. We gathered for the purpose of asking God to redeem the people and the land and to repent on behalf of the people of Texas for (1) innocent blood that was shed at the Village Creek Massacre in Arlington, Texas in 1841, and (2) the broken treaty of Bird's Fort (pre-Arlington) of 1843.

To read a brief historical background you can go to Appendix One.

In response to my prophetic auditory vision and years of spiritual mapping, it was determined that the Lord was calling us to a time of repentance for the shedding of innocent blood and broken covenant. Several prophetic, reconciliatory gatekeeping acts were performed by the leading of God's Spirit. Leaders from Texas and Oklahoma apologized to each other to end any division between Texas and Oklahoma. Dallas Pastors and Leaders (backed up by Tarrant County intercessors) apologized to Tarrant County Pastors and Leaders (backed up by Dallas County intercessors) and vice versa. All the leaders and intercessors shared the Lord's Supper. The group was almost 50-50 from Dallas and Tarrant County. Over half of the group had generational ties to Native Americans. I dipped wooden stakes which would be placed in the ground at Village Creek and

Bird's Fort into the communal cup representing the blood of Jesus that atones for all sin.

At Village Creek, Jay Swallow and I apologized to each other on behalf of the Anglos and Native Americans. We started the stake into the ground followed by each person taking a turn at driving the stake into the ground. Oil was poured over the stake, some bread, and the wine. A fistful of dirt was exchanged. Jay Swallow commissioned me to the apostolic role of caring for this land that has now been redeemed. I, in turn, shared the land with Jay as a sign of our mutual care and responsibility as God's stewards. The dirt was returned to the land. At Bird's Fort, the same prophetic acts were performed. As we did we asked the Lord to purify the area – especially the Trinity River because along the river there had been a spirit of death ever since the Village Creek Massacre and the broken treaty of Bird's Fort. In recent history, two girls were killed right along the river. One was Amber Hagerman (memorialized by the Amber Alert) on the east side of Arlington and Amy Robinson (kidnapped from a Kroger Store) on the west side. They were both found along the river, so we knew that cleansing had to occur.

You may have seen in Let the Sea Resound video by George Otis Jr. and The Sentinel Group[14] what God did in the Fiji Islands, and how when the Lord began to move there was a transformation of a stream and the reefs. One of the things that happened in Arlington in the June after the Bird's Fort Cleansing was that we had record rainfalls like we'd never seen before. All the creeks, all the tributaries, all the forks of the Trinity overflowed their capacity. We knew in our spirit immediately that the rainfall was tied in with what had been done.

During the annual meeting of the International Coalition of Apostles (ICA) in December 2004, I heard something I had not heard before. There were testimonies that during the same months in different states – Colorado, New Mexico, Arizona and others, similar acts had been done, and the rainfall in all of those states went way beyond what has ever been seen before in history. There is more water in Arizona and New Mexico now than has ever been recorded in history. That is amazing to me! Now, there is a trend. God is saying, "I will move, and I will show you that I am cleansing." A similar word was given Dr. Chuck Pierce in July 2006 when he declared that we should keep our eyes on and record the location of natural floods for they are a sign of God's coming revival to those regions. We will see more on this in coming chapters.

God has desired to do this act of cleansing all along but He was waiting for His priests, His agents of change in the world to take up their responsibilities as gatekeepers. Imagine what is in store for our world as we line ourselves up properly with the heart and promises of God and release His presence into every aspect of our lives.

## Cleansing the Forks of the Trinity

Here is another example of gatekeeping. Following several meetings of intercessors and pastors at Church of the King in Dallas, I was prompted by the Lord to draw together a small, covert team representing the two counties (Dallas and Tarrant) to journey to the headwaters of each of the four forks of the Trinity River. The work was done primarily in response to the fact that the Dali Lama had been in Dallas and unholy mandala sand creations had been poured into the Trinity – defiling it! Over the last hundred years the river has been continually defiled by things that have been thrown into it -- both physically and spiritually. The Lord said it had to be cleansed. After researching the river and locating the actual sites of the headwaters, the team was put together and a day was set. On November 10, 2004, six of us traveled to the headwaters of the Clear Fork, West Fork, Elm Fork and East Fork of the Trinity River.

At each of the headwaters, we (1) threw salt in the water and called for a purifying of the waters. We declared them free from defilement, (2) poured grape juice, representing the fruit of the vine and the blood of Jesus and declared the river redeemed. We declared that life and fruitfulness would spring forth from the river. There will be no abortion or miscarriage of God's purposes for the land it touches. We declared that Jesus is Lord of the Trinity River, (3) raised a staff over the water and declared the bringing forth of the waters in God's timing, (4) repented for division caused by having other gods before the Almighty God. We personally laid all other gods down and declared the end of idolatry, (5) dipped water from the water and poured it on the ground. We cried out for His presence and rejoiced in God's provision and deliverance, (6) declared that the Trinity River cannot be stopped by anything thrown into the water that is contrary to God's purposes for the river, and (7) nullified false covenants – "Your covenant is over every name that has been named in this river. You are a jealous God. You will claim this river for Yourself."

Within the week following our trip – like the experience at Bird's Fort in May, the Trinity River and all its forks received rain and reached record levels without causing damage or loss of life. We were able to watch the Trinity River Authority website. We could study the mileage markers along the river and observed the rate of flow at each marker. It was peaking at the headwaters. Peaking! The Lord told us to watch the salt and the communion wash all the way to the Gulf of Mexico. He cleanses. He purifies.

And God doesn't stop at rivers. God is a God who cleanses us, washes us and purifies us. He is a God who desires us to move and have our being in Him, and He will continually bring us to the point of moving us from that first scene in my vision to the last scene – to seeing something dilapidated transformed into something beautiful. Even in that situation God was showing His mercy. He was laughing with the people and hugging them and helping them even though they were broken down. As He touched them the situation transitioned into beauty. That is your life. It is also this church. It is also this city. It is also this state. It is also this nation. It is something God wants to bring about in the world through gatekeepers who obediently respond to the promptings of God.

### On a Personal Level

Another experience happened on a more personal level. I have a good friend, Tim Tremaine, a former police officer, who has been very active in prayer ministry in the city. One day we spent over two hours together talking and sharing. Most importantly we went into a season of prayer. As we prayed, we began to see visions and hear words from the Lord, and the pictures or visions were similar images even though we had not yet shared them with each other. The pictures were giving definition to each other. In my spirit, I recognized that here was a workplace priest (Tim) and a church priest (myself) that God was using to bring something about in the city. The significant thing is that we saw together visions and words dealing with envy in the city, specifically in the church and in its members.

### Vision of the Spirit of Envy in the City

Envy is based on covetousness. Envy or covetousness is seeing something that somebody else has and wanting to have that for ourselves. We saw the spirit of envy moving as a serpent in our dreams and visions. We started taking authority over it, and as soon as we took authority over it, the Lord began dealing with envy in our own hearts. Both of us began to weep. I had to confess my spirit of envy towards him, and he forgave me and vice versa. I had envied Tim. When we first started working together in prayer, he was so far ahead, and I envied his favor, his knowledge and everything that he knew about prayer. That envy became so obvious, and I repented of it to him, and he embraced me and forgave me. We could see things begin to heal. Then we took authority over envy in the city. Gatekeeping works at a citywide and at a personal level.

The next morning at 3:18 I woke up – wide awake in bed, and I saw a waking vision. I saw in front of me – a glob of heads. I knew they were all heads of warriors. They were not good warriors. The first head reminded me of Genghis Khan. Another head was balding, and it reminded me of Mussolini. All of the heads – there were four or five of them – would open their mouths, and out of their mouths would come another head. And that head would open its mouth and out would come another head. Yet, there were never more than five heads. I shook my head wondering if I was truly seeing what I thought I'd seen. Then the Lord showed me the same picture again. It was very big, but it diminished and diminished and diminished and eventually disappeared.

I said, "Lord, what was that?" And He said that is was the spirit of envy that had been dealt with by Tim and me, and it was leaving.

Here is a definition of envy that God delivered to my heart that morning. He said, "Envy is a spirit that speaks only of itself, is consumed with itself and therefore only propagates itself." That was the image of the vision. Nobody was getting anywhere. You would see one head come out of the next mouth. It would open. Then the next head would be revealed. The entire vision was not a pretty picture, but its message was clear. It diminished and floated away. As a result of those prayers and my night vision the Lord moved through a door I allowed to be opened through forgiveness and radically changed my heart towards Tim and others that the Lord allows to be work alongside. Envy has been dealt a death blow and unity has been released.

Whether at a corporate level such as a city or at the level of an individual's own heart, God desires to move us from chaos to order, from dilapidation to transformation. In the next chapters, we will delve into Nehemiah to seek out the Lord's heart on this issue and one thing you will discover is this – the gates are the key! And those gates will be opened by keys. You and I are the keepers of those keys.

## LET US PRAY

Lord Jesus, open my ears to hear, my eyes to see and my heart to perceive Your ways. Transformation will not come to my nation, state, city or own life through religious systems and the wisdom of man. It will come as I open my heart to You in worship and allow You to use me as a gate and gatekeeper to obediently carry out Your will. You want my life to move from chaos to order. You want my world to be transformed into Your glorious kingdom. I open up my hand to receive from You the keys which will open the gates to coming reign. Amen.

# 3

# Nehemiah: The Profile of a Gatekeeper

*"'The survivors who are left from the captivity in the province are there in great distress and reproach. The wall of Jerusalem is also broken down, and its gates are burned with fire.' So, it was, when I heard these words, that I sat down and wept, and mourned for many days; I was fasting and praying before the God of heaven'"*

(NEHEMIAH 1:3-4).

## A DESIRE FOR TRANSFORMATION

The Lord finished by saying, "Embrace Me, Tom, and help them to embrace Me. Pray for them. Build the walls anew, Nehemiah." This  last phrase from my vision, as I stated earlier set me on a course of studying the book and life of Nehemiah. There are some things that you need to keep in mind during the next few chapters. The Book of Nehemiah took place at a very strategic time in Israel's history. Nehemiah did not show up on the scene until years after the exiles returned from Babylon under the decree of Cyrus. The exile was over and the people of God had returned to their land. According to the Book of Ezra, the exiles had already dealt with the issues of the altar and worship and setting down foundations. But now through Nehemiah there is a further message coming from the heart of the Lord. Something further needs to be done.

Let me for a moment put this into the context of a pastor. As I look out over the flock that God has entrusted to me, I witness three categories of people. First, there are those who do not know the Lord. They are not yet redeemed. They are not walking in a life filled with Jesus. They desperately need the Gospel planted in their hearts. The second group is those who have given their lives to the Lord. They know Him, but they still try to maintain control of their own lives. They love to worship and study, but life is still pretty chaotic and disordered. They desperately need their soul-driven nature to submit to the Spirit of the living God.[15] The third group has also given their lives to the Lord. They love to worship, pray and serve, and even though they would have to admit that struggles still come and go, their goal is to see their lives come into God's full redemptive purpose. They are "change agents" or "gates" that have willingly given up control to God in order for God to bring about a complete transformation of their lives and their environment. They understand that our walk in Jesus does not end when we invite Him into our hearts but when our lives transform into a full maturity in Christ Jesus.

On another level, I can sense the same truth regarding the city where God has planted me. Arlington, Texas is a great place to live, and I am thrilled with what has happened in the city as a result of prayer, worship and cooperation among many of the churches. But, I am not satisfied just to have a great city to live in. I am looking for a transformed city – a city that has laid down foundations of righteousness, holiness and grace in Jesus Christ. The church is strong in Arlington. There are many in the city who are who are redeemed, but that is not enough for me – I'm looking for a redeemed city. I am not looking for the church alone but for a city, that the Lord calls His own. A city, as I stated earlier that is willingly giving control to God in order for Him to bring about a complete transformation of the city. The city and the church will understand and experience that our walk in Jesus does not end when we invite Him into our hearts but when our lives are transformed in Christ Jesus.

## Setting the Stage

Nehemiah took place years after the first exiles had returned to Israel. Israel had been exiled because of the blatant disobedience of the people of covenant. Part of their disobedience had been their idolatry. They had intermarried with the pagan cultures in the region and brought the gods of those nations into Judah – the Southern Kingdom. For national strength and defense, they allied themselves with these same pagan nations – trusting them instead of God. Their systems of justice were corrupted. They trampled people, especially the poor, under their feet. Everything about the nation was out of sync with God's heart. Therefore, as He had warned them through the prophets, God allowed the Babylonians to sweep in and take them captive. Jerusalem was a heap of rubble. The temple was ransacked and destroyed. For eighty years they remained in Babylon until the Lord used Cyrus of Persia to declare an edict of release.

The first exiles returned in 538 BC under the leadership of Zerubbabel. When they returned to the destroyed lands of Judah and Jerusalem, the very first thing that Zerubbabel did was to reestablish worship. He set up an altar. He began to offer sacrifices unto the Lord again. The people began to gather for worship and to seek the Lord's face. They then turned to the process of rebuilding the temple. Ezra records the event:

"When the builders laid the foundation of the temple of the LORD, the priests stood in their apparel with trumpets, and the Levites, the sons of Asaph, with cymbals, to praise the LORD, according to the ordinance of David king of Israel. And they sang responsively, praising and giving thanks to the LORD:

'For He is good,

For His mercy endures forever toward Israel.'

Then all the people shouted with a great shout, when they praised the LORD, because the foundation of the house of the LORD was laid" (Ezra 3:10-11).

The temple was ultimately finished in 515 BC. It was built under extreme persecution by surrounding peoples and even by those who had remained in the land during the exile. But under the prophetic exhortations of Haggai and Zechariah the work was completed. The rebuilt temple was considered greatly inferior to Solomon's Temple – so much so that the people, when they saw it finished, wept in mourning. The prophet even said that there was mixed weeping. They were weeping for joy that worship had been established, but weeping in grief that the temple was not of the quality that they knew would honor God.

Nearly sixty years later a second set of exiles returned from Babylon, and gradually more people returned to the land. Between the time of the first and second exiles another story unfolded – the story of Esther. It took place in the same city, in the same citadel that Nehemiah would live in – in Shushan or Suza. Fourteen years after the second exiles returned, Nehemiah came on the scene.

## The Heart of Nehemiah

Nehemiah is a gatekeeper. He is a keeper of the keys. As we see his story unfold we will observe the profile of a gatekeeper. Let's begin with his name. "Nehemiah" is formed from two Hebrew words. The first is "nachum" which means "to breathe strongly; by implication, to be sorry, i.e. (in a favorable sense) to pity, console or (reflexively) rue; or (unfavorably) to avenge (oneself)." [16] It can also be translated as "comfort or repent." The second part of Nehemiah is the Hebrew word "Yah" – the sacred name of the Lord. Nehemiah literally means "Yahweh (the LORD) comforts." Interestingly, the comfort comes through the process of repentance.

The Lord desires to comfort His people, but He will bring about that comfort or ease through repentance. What brings people into restoration, rebuilding and transformation is repentance – a changing of our minds in response to God's favor, mercy and goodness.

Sometime during November and December of 446 BC, Nehemiah was in the citadel in Shushan (Suza). His brother, Hanani and some of his friends had returned to Suza with a report from Jerusalem. Their report is recorded in Nehemiah 1, verse 3.

"The survivors who are left from the captivity in the province are there in great distress and reproach" (They are speaking about the people back in Judah). The wall of Jerusalem is also broken down, and its gates are burned with fire" (Emphasis mine).

I find it extremely troubling that even though the exiles had been back in Judah for many years, nothing had been done about restoring the walls of Jerusalem. Nothing. There are probably a couple of good reasons for that. For one, Jerusalem and the surrounding region was still considered a province of Persia and therefore they could not legally do anything unless Artaxerxes II gave them permission. Putting up walls around a city is a very strong sign of protection and willingness to fight for the people within the wall – not necessarily a healthy thing for a puppet nation or a puppet province to do. It would signal to King Artaxerxes, "We are ready to fight. We are going to take back what is ours." So, no walls had been rebuilt.

Secondly, notice what is missing from Hanani's report. There is no mention of the temple. There is no mention of worship or the sacrifices. Why not? Was worship going on? Were the priests carrying out their daily sacrifices? Possibly, but I have to believe that if their faith was strong in the Lord that there would have been at least an attempt to clean up the city. The report from Hanani speaks of things still in a broken and burned-out state.

The clue may rest in Haggai when the prophet has to exhort the people: "Then the word of the LORD came by Haggai the prophet, saying, 'Is it time for you yourselves to dwell in your paneled houses, and this temple to lie in ruins?' Now therefore, thus says the LORD of hosts: 'Consider your ways'" (Haggai 1:3-5)! Haggai had to rouse the exiles out of selfishness into rebuilding the temple. Now that the temple had been built, had they returned to their own lives, plans and selfishness?

Or was this an issue of shame? The temple was built, but there must have been such shame from the fact that it no longer had glory of Solomon. It wasn't worth mentioning. It's kind of like going back on vacation to see your childhood home, and your childhood home doesn't look anything like it did when you were growing up in it. It used to look like a mansion, and now it looks small and insignificant or it's missing altogether. It is no longer considered important.

What is most amazing about Hanani's report is the response that Nehemiah gave to it. His response was immediate. The Scripture says he sat down. He wept and he mourned for many days. That was his only response. Nehemiah sat down and he wept and he mourned for many days.

We have all been in that place. Weeping or wailing begins to be released in your heart when you realize that somehow what God had determined for your life is no longer there. Why do we mourn at a funeral? Why do we mourn when we see part of our family broken apart by death or divorce? We mourn because something we had considered a promise of God seems forever lost or destroyed. Nehemiah's reaction was immediate mourning and weeping over the fact that Jerusalem – the City of God – David's City – the City of Zion was no longer in the place where God desired it to be as His city.

We need to get a little personal here because we really should have the same response. I'm not speaking about Jerusalem now. I'm speaking about our response regarding Arlington, or Fort Worth or whatever city you live in. We should say, "Lord, this city is nowhere near what we know Your intentions are for the city." It refers also to larger areas such as our state or nation.

You can walk through the city and see that this cannot possibly be God's plan for the city. If God was in charge of our city, what would it look like? Before anything can change, we, as gatekeepers and gates must come to the place of weeping and mourning for our city. We haven't reached that point yet. I believe God is looking for a Nehemiah to fall on his or her face in mourning and weeping over the city. Our spirit, filled with repentance, should weep over the city. Nehemiah was passionate about his city. Where is our passion for our city?

<u>Out of Darkness into Light, Out of Chaos into Order</u>
Let's go to another person in this story. Nehemiah is the son of Hachaliah. This name is also a compound name. The last part of the name, Hachaliah, like Nehemiah, is "Yah" – The Lord God. The first part of the name comes from "chakliyl" which means "to be dark; darkly flashing (only of the eyes)."[17] Hachaliah can literally mean "the darkness of God." Nehemiah was born of a father whose name meant "the darkness of God," and Nehemiah's name means "the comfort of God." Just think on that for a

while. I personally picture, whether it is historical or not, Hachaliah's father and mother, as Hachaliah is born, weeping over the fact that they have left the City of God. Hebrew babies were named after what the parents were experiencing in that moment from God. All they could think of was, "We are in darkness. We are experiencing the darkness of God." The Israelites literally felt that God had left them. The Ark of the Covenant had been taken; the temple was destroyed and therefore God was also gone. The word for the season was Ichabod.

Then she named the child Ichabod, saying, "The glory has departed from Israel!" because the ark of God had been captured and because of her father-in-law and her husband. And she said, "The glory has departed from Israel, for the ark of God has been captured" (1 Samuel 4:21-22)

The people believed that there was nothing but darkness and godlessness in their midst. But something must have been placed in Hachaliah's heart for him to name his son – the comfort of God.

## A GATEKEEPER KNOWS GOD INTIMATELY

Nehemiah, who had never lived in Jerusalem, had surely heard the stories of the city, the magnificence of Solomon's temple, the magnificence of what they had left behind. He had heard also about the problems, the sins, the issues, the failings that had led his people into an exiled experience. He also had an awareness of the covenant mercy of God. It wasn't something he just heard about through the stories of past generations. Nehemiah's understanding of God's covenant mercy must have come from his own experience of the Lord. He obviously had a living relationship with God, which is demonstrated by the prayers that he lifted up to heaven.

The profile of a gatekeeper is revealed through his prayers. When Nehemiah heard about the "torn-up state" of Jerusalem he sat down. He wept. He mourned. His went into an extended time of fasting and prayer. His prayers are summarized in Nehemiah 1:5-11.

And I said: "I pray, LORD God of heaven, O great and awesome God, You who keep Your covenant and mercy with those who love You and observe Your commandments, please let Your ear be attentive and Your eyes open, that You may hear the prayer of Your servant which I pray before You now, day and night, for the children of Israel Your servants, and confess the sins of the children of Israel which we have sinned against You. Both my father's house and I have sinned. We have acted very corruptly against You, and have not kept the commandments, the statutes, nor the ordinances which You commanded Your servant Moses. Remember, I pray, the word that You commanded Your servant Moses, saying, 'If you are unfaithful, I will scatter you among the nations; but if you return to Me, and keep My commandments and do them, though some of you were cast out to the farthest part of the heavens, yet I will gather them from there, and bring them to the place which I have chosen as a dwelling for My name.' Now these are Your servants and Your people, whom You have redeemed by Your great power, and by Your strong hand. O Lord, I pray, please let Your ear be attentive to the prayer of Your servant, and to the prayer of Your servants who desire to fear Your name; and let Your servant prosper this day, I pray, and grant him mercy in the sight of this man."

## A GATEKEEPER HONORS GOD

Nehemiah's Prayer has three very significant parts to it. **In the first part of this prayer Nehemiah declared the awesomeness and greatness of God.** It is obviously a declaration from Nehemiah's heart. Nehemiah declared that it is God and God alone Who is almighty and awesome and all powerful. He immediately went to the heart of the issue and declared Who God is in His presence.

Here are some of the things that Nehemiah mentioned before God:

### God is the Keeper of Covenant

We know that God is the Keeper of His Covenant. The people of Israel had broken the covenant, but God had not broken the covenant. God's covenant is still in place. Nehemiah declared that. In paraphrasing his thoughts, Nehemiah said to the people what God had said to him: "Even though you might be scattered to the very farthest point of the heavens, I will bring you back because I love you. I'm the One Who scattered you there, but I will bring you back. Even when you have to receive judgment, don't forget that I am the awesome God, I am the Keeper of the Covenant. I am the One Who established My love for you. I'm the One Who loves you with an undying love. I will never give up on you."

We have to declare that in our own lives. We will never give up. When we look at situations that are broken down and out of sync and we know that in the eyes of God things are not right; we can still hear the Lord God say, "I am the Keeper of the Covenant, and I will never stop seeking you. I will come after you with My love."

## God is a God of mercy.

God is a God Who shows mercy and faithfulness. He is a God Who does not mark iniquities against people. You say if He doesn't mark iniquities against His people, then why are the people in Babylon in the first place. God didn't mark those iniquities against them. The people were disobedient to Him, and He had to move them into a place where they would once again acknowledge that He is a forgiving God.

The issue with the Israelites is that they had completely lost contact with a compassionate, merciful God. They had forgotten that He could forgive them of the sins that they had committed. All they could concentrate on was the fact that they wanted to do their own thing. So, God had to move them into a wilderness, into a place of suffering just to wake them up to the fact again that He is merciful and that He will restore them.

## God is a God who brings forth light!

It is truly amazing to me that Nehemiah, one of those people born in exile, born away from Jerusalem, would have such and intimate, personal relationship with God. In the midst of the darkness, God brought forth light to Nehemiah. He will bring forth a relationship even when we with our natural eyes think it is totally impossible. Here was a man born in exile, born in the darkness of one of Israel's blackest moments, but one who has an intimate, powerful relationship with God's heart; and so, in his darkest times, God brought forth his faith, brought forth a declaration, brought forth a life of comfort and repentance; and Nehemiah, born out of the darkness of God, became the comfort of God. Nehemiah, himself, the leader of the people, began to repent and to confess his sins.

## A GATEKEEPER LEADS A LIFE OF REPENTANCE

In Nehemiah's case, it was God's goodness that led to his repentance.

"⁴Or do you despise the riches of His goodness, forbearance, and longsuffering, not knowing that the goodness of God leads you to repentance" (Romans 2:4)? God's goodness went into Nehemiah's heart in such a way that it brought forth a need to respond with repentance – saying, "God, what have we done?"

We don't have any record of this, but I wonder – is it possible that a spirit of repentance never fell upon the people of Israel that had returned from the exile? Had they ever come to the point where they realized that they had indeed sinned against God? You can go through a real struggle in your life. Everything seems to be going downhill, and you wonder when God is going to rescue you out of it. And all of a sudden, a blessing comes. God brings you out of the situation. You are home again. Everything is good. The most important question in that moment is – has an evaluation of your relationship with God taken place? Has there been a time of confession, repentance and a desire to give Him full control. Did that happen with the Israelites who came to Jerusalem earlier or did most of them just repack their bags and go home – relieved that their exile was over? Is it possible that the people in Judah never worked through a season of repentance and renewing relationship with God, so God in His faithfulness brought repentance forth through Nehemiah?

**This is the second part of Nehemiah's prayer**. It became a confession of sins. And it came from a heart that knew God's heart. Nehemiah pleaded with God to open His eyes and ears and to be attentive to the prayers that he was offering up to Him.

Nehemiah's relationship with God was being revealed. "Lord, would You please. I know that You are the mighty God of the entire universe, but for just a moment, would You put Your ear down to my heart?" Here is a person with a personal relationship with God. He is not considering God to be a vague, powerful force out there that might hear us. No! Nehemiah says, "Would You bring Your ear close to me? I need to say something to You. I need to talk to You person to person. I need to speak into Your ear. I need to look into Your eyes."

What an amazing relationship Nehemiah must have had with the Lord! There was genuine sincerity coming out of Nehemiah's heart. He was pleading day and night for Israel. He was pleading for the Jews, but most importantly, he was confessing their sins.

If Nehemiah's prayers, according to the text, lasted several days, just imagine him pondering over all the sins that his father or grandfather had relayed to him – the same sins that God Himself was now revealing to Nehemiah's heart. When God gets close to you, He's going to hear you, but, guess what – you are also going to hear Him. You are going to hear God's heart – His brokenness. Nehemiah heard the torn heart of God – the realization that His chosen people had not kept the covenant. It was a covenant based on love and mercy, and they had abandoned it. They had abandoned God.

This must have been a truly heart wrenching time for Nehemiah. I know many of us have been in that same situation. You can be praying and the Lord will begin to drop things on your heart that will just wrench your heart. All you can do is cry, "Oh, God, I'm sorry I did that!" When you are in that season, you don't say it that mildly. You may be on your hands and your knees. You might be on your face crying or just stunned. "Lord, I cannot believe that I have sinned that way – that I betrayed You, or forsook You or didn't trust You, Lord, that I did that to my family or I said that when I shouldn't have. Lord, please forgive me." When God's goodness starts coming upon us, there is a move of repentance that is heart wrenching. This experience was excruciating for Nehemiah.

Even more important than the fact that Nehemiah confessed the sins of his fathers is the fact that he included himself. Why did he do that? Nehemiah wasn't there when all those sins were committed. He was born in Suza long after all of this took place. He wasn't there when Judah sinned nearly a hundred years earlier! Nehemiah wasn't living in Judah. He wasn't even living in the time of David and Solomon and all the kings after that. Nehemiah didn't worship any false gods. He didn't set up any Asheroth poles. He didn't do anything else that all the prophets had told them they were doing. Nehemiah had done none of that as far as we know. None of it! And yet he confessed. He identified himself with what they had done and acknowledged that he was a part of it because he realized he was of the same spirit and of the same blood.

This isn't a new thought. Let me give you an example. "Lord, God, I have sinned in exactly the same way Adam sinned." I just identified with Adam's sin. I didn't commit the same sin. I didn't go pick fruit off the forbidden tree. I haven't even been in that garden, but my attitude and my heart is the same. I am a part of Adam's sin. I have sinned just as Adam sinned because I am of the same spirit and of the same heritage.

Nehemiah may not have done any of those things. He must have committed his own sins, but not those. Yet, he confessed, "Both my father's house and I have sinned."

It is called identificational repentance.

As we who are citizens of the United States of America look at the sins in our own lives, our own households, our own workplaces, our own city, our own state, or our own nation, we have to realize that we must confess any of these sins that have been committed in the United States even though we have not committed them. We are a part of those sins because they are a part of our heritage, and we must clean them out of our lives.[18] These sins are passed on from generation to generation. At some point, the Spirit of the Lord needs a Nehemiah or needs you to step up and say:

"God, there has been a trend in my family for the last four generations. It stops here. It doesn't stop here because I am declaring it. It stops here because I confess that I, too, am sinful of it. I have allowed this sin to sleep in my bed. I have allowed it to stay in my house. I have allowed it to live in my city. I have allowed it to live in my nation. No more, Lord. I plead with You, put Your ear down to my heart, and listen to me on this. Would You hear all of my pleadings? I am sorry for the sins my fathers and I have committed against You."

I truly believe that as we move in identificational repentance with all sincerity, the things that were patterns – divorce, addictions, perversions, lying, deceit, anxiety, fears, and all the tools of the enemy will no longer be patterns. If any of these iniquities have gone through your family, it is time for you, Nehemiah, to stand up and say, "Wait a minute; I am coming to You, God, to confess this sin."

It doesn't help to get in the highest place in your house and yell and scream at Satan and say, "No more!" That is not where the issue starts. The issue starts between you and God. God says, "Wait a minute. Let's clean the slate all the way down to the bottom, and this includes you."

Confess the sin. Don't rationalize it. Man, I love doing that. God will speak something in my heart, and I will think, "Lord, I didn't do that. I don't think I've done that." See, I've begun to rationalize. He doesn't want me to rationalize it. Just confess it. He puts it in our heart to confess it. Be done with it. Grab that thing and pull it out roots and everything and hold it up before the Lord and say, "I have sinned. This is my sin. I put it before You. Lord, according to Your mercy, forgive me." And He says, "If you confess your sins, I Who am faithful and just will forgive you from all of your sins. I will cleanse you from all unrighteousness" (1 John 1:9). "ALL unrighteousness" includes all the generations – past, present and future.

I strongly believe that as you and I confess the sins of our families, the true act of transformation begins to unfold. As pastors or other representatives confess the sins of past and present generations, things which have hampered the transformation of the city are broken off. Amen! Doesn't that excite you? You can do that in your workplace. If there are iniquitous patterns there, just begin to say, "Lord, I'm in here. I am an employee here. I've got to take responsibility here. I ask for forgiveness for the sins of my fathers and myself." Don't wait for the boss. Quit pointing at the boss and saying, "If we could just get a new boss, a Christian boss; if we could just get a Christian president..." That is not the issue. The issue is that someone who has the conviction of God about revealed sins will confess them and ask God's forgiveness for them.

In the previous chapter I shared about the Village Creek Reconciliation. I have been out to the site of the massacre of innocent Native American women and children with pastors and leaders and intercessors. We wept over the sins that have been revealed to us. We have confessed them. I had nothing to do with the massacre. None of the people who went with us did. Yet, something has changed in the atmosphere since we asked forgiveness for the atrocity that was committed in our city. Ask the Lord to bring that spirit upon you – a spirit of repentance. It is not a dangerous thing. It is God's heart. God is restoring Village Creek completely out of His love and out of His desire to bring everything back to its original place, to His perfect intentions. God is waiting patiently for us to cry out for His faith.

## A GATEKEEPER STANDS IN THE GAP

**And finally, the third part of Nehemiah's prayer is a call for God to remember.** Nehemiah takes the Lord all the way back to Moses. Can you hear Moses up on Mt. Sinai? The Lord was so upset with the people of Israel that He said in effect, "Moses, just get out of the way. I'm going to blast these people off the face of this mountain, and I am going to start a new nation with you as a leader."[19] Now, being a pastor and a pastor of the city, I think Moses might have been momentarily tempted to say, "Do it! Let's get this over with." But he didn't. Moses stood in the gap for the children of Israel. He said, "Wait a minute, God! You are the One Who made this covenant. You are the One Who made this people. These are Your people, not mine. (This is Your city, God, not mine). Remember Your covenant with them."

What was God's response to Moses? God changed His mind. Listen to this. Goodness leads to repentance; therefore, God's goodness leads us to repentance. In a like manner, I believe that God's goodness in us leads Him to repentance. God changed His mind. He says to me as a pastor: "Back off, Tom, I've had enough of Arlington." I have to say, "No, Lord, I'm sorry. You cannot destroy the city yet. You may want to send judgment on the city, but first remember that You made the covenant with the first settlers. You planted the city here."

I believe God changes His mind. I believe He has changed His mind about judging Arlington. He has changed His mind about judging your city. There is much more confessing and repenting to do, but I believe God is changing His mind.

Listen to this passage of Nehemiah's prayer from The Message by Eugene Peterson.[20] This is Nehemiah 1:7-11. Nehemiah is speaking to God:

"We've treated you like dirt: We haven't done what you told us, haven't followed your commands, and haven't respected the decisions you gave to Moses your servant. All the same, remember the warning you posted to your servant Moses: "If you betray me, I'll scatter you to the four winds, but if you come back to me and do what I tell you, I'll gather up all these scattered peoples from wherever they ended up and put them back in the place I chose to mark with my Name.'

"Well, there they are--your servants, your people whom you so powerfully and impressively redeemed. O Master, listen to me, listen to your servant's prayer--and yes, to all your servants who delight in honoring you--and make me successful today so that I get what I want from the king."

## A GATEKEEPER GAINS FAVOR

This whole process of repentance is leading to the fulfillment of one purpose – so that Nehemiah will have favor with King Artaxerxes. That will come up in the next chapter. What Nehemiah is saying here is that God will judge His people. He reminds God of that. We should remind God of that. "It is in Your power to judge us, God. You can scatter us wherever You want us to be scattered, but You will always put us back into our appointed places."

Listen to this testimony from Acts 17:24-28:

God, who made the world and everything in it, since He is Lord of heaven and earth, does not dwell in temples made with hands. Nor is He worshiped with men's hands, as though He needed anything, since He gives to all life, breath, and all things. And He has made from one blood[ every nation of men to dwell on all the face of the earth, and has determined (this is speaking to you) their preappointed times and the boundaries of their dwellings (God has appointed you to be where you are), so that they (you) should seek the Lord, in the hope that they (you) might grope for Him and find Him, though He is not far from each one of us; for in Him we live and move and have our being, as also some of your own poets have said, "For we are also His offspring.' (emphasis mine)

God has powerfully redeemed us. He has appointed us in a place. He has set up the boundaries of our appointment -- where we live, where we work, our family, and our names. God has appointed all of these things, and He will be faithful to us because of His covenant. God would make Nehemiah's trip to the king successful even though Nehemiah was but a cupbearer. Favor would be granted by Nehemiah's awesome God, and Judah would be restored. What an amazing story!

Can this happen in or own lives? Yes, when our hearts line up with God's heart and He is attentive to our cries, God's strength and provision are released. The enemy may come against us, but he will not prevail. God's hand is moving. It is time for us to step up as Nehemiah's in our homes, in our churches, in our cities, and in the marketplace and expect God to bring the restoration He has promised.

How do you line up your heart with God's heart? Just ask the Lord to be attentive to the cries of your heart. Say, "Lord, would You put Your ear right here (on my heart), and let me share with You what is on my heart. Then begin to confess the sins, not just your sins, but also the sins of your father, your supervisor, your mayor. Begin to confess what You know is out of alignment with His purposes. He will bring promised restoration. He will rebuild walls. He will restore relationships. He will do all of that by His mighty hand. We may not see it at the end of our generation but it will happen. In the passage, we have read in Nehemiah, it all started in that one moment when Nehemiah cried out in Suza pleading with God for mercy.

LET US PRAY.

Father, we ask that You release over Your people Your Spirit, Your goodness and Your comfort that leads us to repentance. Open our eyes, Lord. If we saw something happening in our parents and we see it happening again in us, we need to confess. Lord, if we see something happening with our kids that happened with us and our parents, we need to confess. If we see something happening in our homes, our workplace, our church or in our city, dear Lord, we need to confess. We ask that Your Spirit reveal to us as You revealed to Nehemiah the sins of the people so we can stand in the gap as Your priests, as the intercessors that You have called us to be. Lord, we ask for forgiveness on behalf of past generations and of ourselves. Heal us. Restore us. Rebuild the walls that You, the King of Glory may come in and be truly enthroned in our midst. To You be all the glory and all the honor and all the praise in Jesus' name.

# 4

# The Cupbearer

*"For I was the king's cupbearer"*

(NEHEMIAH 1:11B)

## GOD'S FAVOR RELEASED TO A GATEKEEPER

The Lord was positioning Nehemiah as a gatekeeper or gate through which He could bring His kingdom. We will look in more detail at that gatekeeping role in coming chapters but for now let's continue to examine the story of Nehemiah. Nehemiah went into a season of prayer and fasting in order that he might find favor with King Artaxerxes.

When our hearts line up with God's heart, God's favor, strength and provision will be released. The enemy may come against us, but he will not prevail. God's hand is moving. When you are in your home, workplace, church, city or nation and you line up your heart with God's, believe me, God will begin to move through that channel of your heart to change things for His kingdom. Nehemiah lined up his heart with God, and he received God's favor. By going to the almighty King, he gained the attention of the earthly King.

## God's Surprise Strategy

The Lord grants His favor and releases His restoration work through people we oftentimes would consider insignificant. Consider the shepherds of Bethlehem. Talking about insignificant people being used by God! The first people to receive the good news of Jesus and the first ones to worship Him were considered the outcasts of society in Israel. They were dirty. They were common. They were uneducated. They were not considered valuable by the religious society, and yet God chose them.

And then God brought magi from the outside the Holy Land, from the east, to be the second people to see His Son. God is saying in this hour, "Regardless of your station in life, if you seek My face and My heart, I will use you in the strategies which will unlock My kingdom on the earth. I will put you into places that you never thought you could be used before."

This is Nehemiah's story:

## The Cupbearer

Nehemiah was a cupbearer for the king.

Let me share with you a little bit about cupbearers.

Cup bearing was purely a servant role.

There was no honor attached to it.

Most of the time the position was filled by enslaved people. They were searched out, much like Daniel, and lifted up to be used in the courts as servants to the kings and his court. They were there for the king's pleasure.

But even though cup bearing was a servant role, it was a place of high trust. The cupbearer was a server and taster of the king's wine or any other drink he might want to have. Nehemiah, in this case, was the last person to check the wine before it was given to the king. If the drink was bad, tainted or poisoned the cupbearer would taste it first. The cupbearer was one who was considered expendable. He was expected to serve and to give up his life on behalf of the king.

But the cupbearer was more than a check for poisonous drinks. Nehemiah 2:1 states that Nehemiah was the one who took the wine to the king. The king should not have to ask for a drink. Nehemiah had to have such a relationship with the king that he knew when the king wanted something to drink. When I go into a restaurant, I don't care if my glass is empty or not. The waitress or waiter should assume that I am getting thirsty and want more tea. Just come and fill my glass. Until I pay the bill and leave the restaurant, fill up the glass. That is similar to the kind of the relationship Nehemiah had with the king. Nehemiah was to know when the king was thirsty. Nehemiah was to know what the king preferred to drink. If on Monday he saw a wine set before the king that was not the kind the king drinks on Mondays, Nehemiah had better get the right wine before it was served to the king. He had to know the preference of the king. He had to know the king.

If you are going to know the king you are going to have to spend some time in his presence. You know his whims. You know his desires. You know his quirks. You know his strengths. You know when to serve him. The cupbearer, therefore, was really in a trusted relationship with the king.

The cupbearer in many ways was also an informal source of counsel to the king. It is conceivable that as the cupbearer brought the wine before the king the king would lean over, receive his drink and say, "What do you hear in my kingdom? Is there any treachery in my kingdom? Is all well?" In other words, the king knew that the cupbearer was in a place where he was available to inside information about his kingdom.

So, there was a trusted relationship between the king and the cupbearer that did not exist with any other person in the court. But along with this trust came a great burden. If the cupbearer failed in any of these tasks; if Nehemiah failed at getting the cup at the right time, or brought the wrong wine at the wrong time; if he failed to give counsel or gave wrong counsel, it would mean certain imprisonment, if not death. We can go back several centuries to the story of Joseph. While Joseph was in the dungeon, the king of Egypt's cupbearer and baker joined him as fellow prisoners. They were imprisoned because they had done something that displeased the king. Do you remember that Joseph interpreted their dreams? The baker subsequently lost his head and the cupbearer went back to his position of trusted servanthood. Joseph told the cupbearer to mention him on his release, but he forgot. When the king was greatly troubled by his dreams and counsel was needed – notice that it was not the wise men of the kingdom, it was not the great scholars or magicians of the kingdom, but it was the cupbearer who gave the "key" advice.

You can picture the scene. The cupbearer is bringing the cup of wine to the king, possibly even trembling a little a bit because he realizes that he could go back to the dungeon on this one. But he says, "I remember my faults this day. I met someone in the dungeon who I know can interpret your dreams." And in that moment favor was released on Joseph. The cupbearer of the king played a very key role in God's plan of elevating Joseph.

We have a similar scenario with Nehemiah. Nehemiah is now in this key and God-appointed position of cupbearer. And it is God-appointed position. Nehemiah didn't show up at the king's door in Shushan and say, "I'd like to sign on for cupbearer." He was just pulled out of the ranks of enslaved people. Nobody is brought into a position except by the appointment of God Himself. Whether you are the president of the United States or King Artaxerxes or King Artaxerxes' cupbearer, God is the One who brings forth the appointment and the anointing of that position.

Whatever position you are in at this moment,
> you can be an employee or an employer,
> you can be a plumber or a college student,
> you can be an assembly plant worker, a nurse,
> a teacher, a professor, or an engineer,

it makes no difference what your position is, you are there as an appointed servant of God. And an appointed servant of God, the King, will faithfully (as a trusted servant) carry out whatever the King desires. God is releasing His kingdom purposes through us. God is placing each of us into a Joseph position, an Esther position, a Nehemiah position or a Paul position. As we seek His face and serve Him in worship, God will position us for kingdom work. Never underestimate what God may be doing through you. Never underestimate or scoff at your job or position.

I can remember years ago how I did not consider myself very important in God's overall scheme of things. I was "just" a pastor of a small church wanting to faithfully proclaim His Gospel and disciple

His children. I had received a prophetic word that I would prophesy and pray over national, state and local leaders, but I pretty much dismissed it as impossibility. However, four years later on my first trip to Honduras, I was asked to prophesy to the highest ranking general over the Honduran armed forces. On the next visit, I prophesied over the First Lady of Honduras. In the last couple of years, I have been given the favor of directly praying and speaking into the life of the Mayor of Arlington, several city council members and other city leaders. The Lord has honored me by allowing me to prophesy to Governors and our Attorney General.

I could share many testimonies of members from this "small Church" that are ministering to...

Hollywood producers,

State officials,

Corporation leaders,

City leaders,

International leaders, and

Bosses.

And it's not just about ministering to big name people. God positions us to be there for a healing prayer, an encouraging word or a timely word of counsel to family members, co-workers, neighbors and friends. Seek God's heart. Line yourself up with His purposes. He has created you as a servant, a priest, an ambassador for His kingdom – regardless of your rank, position or occupation in life. And God will use His divine appointments to change a king's heart and to shift the direction of a nation from chaos into transformation.

## THE CHANGING OF A KING'S HEART

"The king's heart is in the hand of the LORD,

Like the rivers of water; He turns it wherever He wishes" (Proverbs 21:1).

The King's heart is in the hand of the Lord. He turns it wherever He wishes. This is very true. God will turn the heart of the king by His hand. But typically, He is going to use a Nehemiah to get to the heart. He will use someone within the palace to make the change.

So, what position are you in? What king are you going before? What boss? What situation? What city? Every single one of you, regardless of your station in life, will be positioned and anointed by God for transformation.

## IN GOD'S TIMING

So, Nehemiah goes before the king. "And it came to pass in the month of Nisan, in the twentieth year of King Artaxerxes, when wine was before him, that I took the wine and gave it to the king" (Nehemiah 2:1a). It is important here for a moment to understand the timing involved in this process. Nehemiah came before the king in the month of Nisan. Nisan, like the month of Chislev mentioned in first chapter of Nehemiah, is a part of the sacred Jewish calendar. Nisan, also called Abib, is the first month of the year. It is the month designated as the time of Passover, deliverance and First Fruits. It is an extremely crucial month in God's seasons and God's timing. It corresponds to the death and resurrection of our Lord Jesus. It is a "now" time in God's eyes for something to happen. It is time for deliverance. It is time for something new. It's a time to "cross over" into something new. It's time to move out of transition into full apostolic authority.

Nisan takes place four months after Chislev. Let's rehearse the story. Nehemiah is in Shushan and his brothers and friends come to him. He hears the report of the fallen and burnt walls of Jerusalem. He immediately goes into fasting and prayer. The next day, as the cupbearer, he sees some wine in front of the king. He hands him the wine and tells his "sad" story. No, that's not the timing of the story. Four months have passed by. Four months of prayer and fasting. Four months waiting for that moment when the Lord would move upon him. We can't even know for certain if Nehemiah knew what was going to happen as far as him gaining favor with the king. He was just carrying out his duties. And in the fourth month after hearing the news, the cup is before the king. He picks up the cup and approaches the king, but something is different today. Something is very different. He has a long face. He is sad.

"Now I had never been sad in his presence before. Therefore, the king said to me, 'Why is your face sad, since you are not sick? This is nothing but sorrow of heart.' So, I became dreadfully afraid, and said to the king, 'May the king live forever'" (Nehemiah 1:1b-3a)!

Now, folks, this is really significant. If you are going to be a cupbearer, it's not only important that you give the king the wine at the right time and give him some informal counsel; As a cup bearer, you need to approach the king in the right state of mind. You don't come into the king's presence sad. You come in with honor and dignity. There is to be no focus on you at all. The focus is supposed to be on the king, not on the cupbearer. If you come in with a sad face and you never had been that way before, guess who's watching? Everyone, but especially the king. In the next few moments the rest of Nehemiah's life would be defined for him. He is either going to have favor or he is going to end up in prison or headless. You don't come into the king's presence like Nehemiah came in, unless you are coming in with a testimony in your heart from the Spirit of God that today is the day and now is the moment.

"'Why should my face not be sad, when the city, the place of my fathers' tombs, lies waste, and its gates are burned with fire?'

Then the king said to me, 'What do you request?'

So, I prayed to the God of heaven" (Nehemiah 2:3b-4).

## GOD'S FAVOR

And in that moment – in God's timing – and as a response to prayer and fasting, God's favor and Artaxerxes' favor is released on Nehemiah. Favor is an act of kindness that is granted to another person out of the goodwill of the giver. Favor is granted as a gift.

In the year 2000, I was meeting with pastors of the city on a regular basis for prayer and fellowship. Even though I had a strong desire to pray for the city I considered myself again as "just one of the pastors." I did not think my opinion counted and I was rarely approached for ideas or strategies. One afternoon I attended a meeting hosting by Dallas County pastors. The speaker was Bishop Bart Pierce of Rock City Church in Baltimore. It was a powerful teaching. At the end of the meeting Bishop Pierce invited all of us to front for ministry. I anticipated a great outpouring. I was about halfway down the line and the persons to my left were being touched powerfully as Bishop Pierce ministered to them. They were literally "falling like flies." When he came to me I reached out my hands to him. He took my hands and simply spoke, "The favor of God and the favor of man" and he went to the next person. That was it. I personally was disappointed and moments later headed home.

The next day I was at a regular prayer meeting of the city pastors when I was approached by the presiding pastor of the group. He asked me to serve on the leadership team for the group which was going to meet later that week. I was caught off guard but accepted. When I arrived at that meeting the other three pastors turned to me almost in unison and asked me to oversee the gathering of intercessors from the city for prayer. In that moment, I knew that the favor of God and man had come – totally to my surprise. Out of that moment came Arlington Prayer Net – a gathering of intercessory leaders from the city – and eventually River of Intercession – a gathering of apostolic intercessory leaders from the Dallas-Fort Worth region.

God was granting me favor so that I could serve as a key or gate to the area in which I life. As I continued to move in that role the Lord increased favor and influence. I eventually was invited to serve as a regional director (from Texas) on the Oklahoma Apostolic Prayer Network. The Lord instructed me to start a similar network in North Texas called the Trinity Apostolic Prayer Network. And in June of 2007 I was commissioned as coordinator of the Texas Apostolic Prayer Network. As such I was given a "key" to the state of Texas.

I could give many testimonies of how God has literally dropped favor on this insignificant pastor (cupbearer) from a small church in the heart of the Dallas-Fort Worth Metroplex. And since it is favor – all the glory goes to the Giver – the Lord Jesus Christ.

## WHAT'S ON YOUR HEART?

Folks, I don't know what the Lord is going to put upon your heart or what you will say when He uses you in His kingdom. Nehemiah's life was on the line. I don't think he would have said, "Oh, don't worry about it, King. I'm just sad. I've heard some bad news from back home. Here's your wine."

No, he shared his heart. When there comes a moment, especially after a lot of prayer, that a co-worker or a family member asks you "What's on your heart?" the last thing you need to talk about is the weather, last night's game, the children or grandchildren or what you ate last night. At that moment, God's favor is opening a door. Oh, there is risk involved, but the door is opening and God's favor is resting on you.

In the moment that favor is bestowed, we need to come into boldness and share our heart. Nehemiah's life was on the line, but God released His favor to Nehemiah. Instead of the gallows, Nehemiah received an acknowledgment of the sorrow. Not only an acknowledgement of the sorrow but the king's question, "What do you request?" I can only imagine the relief, shock or burst of faith that came into Nehemiah's heart. And his next move is his most strategic. He prayed. Before answering he prayed.

"And I said to the king, 'If it pleases the king, and if your servant has found favor in your sight, I ask that you send me to Judah, to the city of my fathers' tombs, that I may rebuild it'" (Nehemiah 2:5).

How awesome is this moment. How inconceivable! The king of the most powerful nation of that time in history was asking the cupbearer what he wanted. What kind of favor is this? Can we be so bold as to have a desire that this would happen in our lives? That a king would ask a servant of an enslaved foreign culture, "What do you request?" A key was given to Nehemiah to unlock the destiny of Jerusalem!

And as I mentioned earlier, Nehemiah, still humbled in the presence of God, prayed. Now folks, we have to be clear on some prayer ministry etiquette here. This was not a situation where Nehemiah could say, "Dear king, would you hold that thought for a moment so I can go and spend some time in the prayer closet. Then I'll come back to you with an answer." Nehemiah had spent four months in the prayer closet. He knew exactly what the Lord's heart was for Jerusalem. He knew exactly what to ask. All he was doing now at this point was what we call praying a "breath prayer." "Lord God, here's the moment – give me the words."

In Matthew 10:18-20 Jesus was talking to His disciples and warning them of those times when they would be brought before kings. He told them not to worry about what they would say, for the Spirit of God would come upon them and they would speak what God wanted them to speak..." "Lord it's now the moment, come and speak." And He did.

So, in this passage, Nehemiah made his request. It was detailed. It was distinct. It was not general. It was not just dropping things out there and hoping that they fall in the right place. It was what we call in today's prayer movement "a smart bomb." In other words, Nehemiah had on his heart what God had on His heart and there was no doubt about it.

As a result, Nehemiah spoke with confidence. Here was a cupbearer turning into a governor. Nehemiah didn't just ask the king to deal with the Jerusalem situation. Nehemiah, a cup bearer said, "Send me to rebuild Jerusalem!"

There's no evidence that Nehemiah knows how to build.

We have no evidence that he's an engineer.

All we've got is that he knows God,

And this God that Nehemiah knew intimately said "This is what you are to ask of the king – Send me to build the city." There is an attitude in Nehemiah's heart that we can't skip over. He sought God's heart. We need to seek God's heart. We need to be obedient to the tasks that He sets before us. And regardless of our position in life we are not to wait for some other Nehemiah to do the task. Just say, "Lord, show me what You want me to do in my family, in my workplace, in my school, in my neighborhood, and in my city, and I will do it."

I have come to the point where I have few qualms anymore. I know that I am one of the Lord's appointed servants in this city to see the walls of Arlington rebuilt. I am not going to wait for someone else to do it. He has called me to do it. Others will join with me, and I will join others. There will be provision for the task. I don't want the Lord to have to find someone else. You need to come into that same place in your workplace, in your home, or wherever you are.

"Lord you have appointed me to be the Nehemiah in my house, the Nehemiah in my school, the Nehemiah in my workplace. Lord, give me the anointing of your Spirit, line up my heart with your heart and let me know what needs to be done and when it needs to be done. Even if it takes four months from now, five years from now, ten years from now, I want to do it. I will do it, just give me the timing and the words."

And the Lord will do it.

"Then the king said to me (the queen also sitting beside him), 'How long will your journey be? And when will you return?' So, it pleased the king to send me; and I set him a time. Furthermore, I said to the king, 'If it pleases the king, let letters be given to me for the governors of the region beyond the River, that they must permit me to pass through till I come to Judah, and a letter to Asaph the keeper of the king's forest, that he must give me timber to make beams for the gates of the citadel which pertains to the temple, for the city wall, and for the house that I will occupy.' And the king granted them to me according to the good hand of my God upon me. Then I went to the governors in the region beyond the River, and gave them the king's letters. Now the king had sent captains of the army and horsemen with me. When Sanballat the Horonite and Tobiah the Ammonite official heard of it, they were deeply disturbed that a man had come to seek the well-being of the children of Israel" (Nehemiah 2:6-10).

Look what favor is on Nehemiah when God's timing is right! Artaxerxes offers no challenge to his request. The door of favor swings wide open. When the Lord is showing His favor, go for it! I really believe that everything Nehemiah asked for, the Lord had put in his heart. He was not asking out of whim. He was asking for what was on God's heart. And the king granted the request according to the good hand of God upon Nehemiah – favor!

Notice the compassion and the tenderness of the king. He didn't even hesitate. While I was praying through and writing this portion, I saw in my spirit the same palace and the same court and the same room where Esther had come before the king years earlier. Is it possible that all those images of Esther were present that day in the king's heart? If so, it is another testimony of the faithfulness of God.

God was in charge. Boldness in the Lord took over and Nehemiah received all that he needed. All that he needed! Nehemiah ended up going to the governors in the region beyond the river. He had letters from the king. But not only letters - the king had sent captains of the army and horsemen along with Nehemiah. He didn't say "So long Nehemiah. We'll see you when you get back." No, Nehemiah had letters. He had the king's blessing. He had an army. He had captains. He had horsemen. He had personal escort. Can you imagine the scene? A cupbearer – an enslaved member of the king's court – with such favor and honor placed on him. You need to imagine it! You need to embrace it! God wants to transform the world you live in and He is calling you in the same way He called a cupbearer named Nehemiah. God, through Artaxerxes, had favored Nehemiah with permission, provision and protection!

## LET US PRAY

Father God, thank you so much that you have called each us. We are your children. We are your ambassadors. We are cupbearers. We are servants. We are also your friends. We seek counsel from you. And Lord you are even willing to seek counsel from us to hear what is on our heart. Lord, we come before You know what the cost will be, but Lord would you please pour Your Spirit into us. Line our hearts up with Your heart and grant us Your favor. Lord, open our eyes to see those strategic moments take place for Your kingdom. Whatever it takes, Lord. We are available. We say yes! Please birth in each of us a spirit and anointing that was upon Nehemiah, Joseph, Esther, Paul and all the rest. To You be the glory and the honor and the power now and forever more. Amen

# 5

## Examining the Walls

*"So, I came to Jerusalem and was there three days. Then I arose in the night, I and a few men with me; I told no one what my God had put in my heart to do at Jerusalem; nor was there any animal with me, except the one on which I rode. And I went out by night through the Valley Gate to the Serpent Well and the Refuse Gate, and viewed the walls of Jerusalem which were broken down and its gates which were burned with fire. Then I went on to the Fountain Gate and to the King's Pool, but there was no room for the animal under me to pass. So, I went up in the night by the valley, and viewed the wall; then I turned back and entered by the Valley Gate, and so returned. And the officials did not know where I had gone or what I had done; I had not yet told the Jews, the priests, the nobles, the officials, or the others who did the work"*

*(Nehemiah 2:11-16)*

### SETTING THE SCENE

Let me remind you of a few facts regarding Nehemiah. In the darkest times—God brought forth faith, life and comfort. Out of the darkness of God

(Hachaliah), the comfort of God (Nehemiah) came forth. Nehemiah – a cupbearer of the king – was an enslaved servant, filled with God's Spirit, who responded to news about Jerusalem's condition with prayer and fasting. Nehemiah received favor before the king and was sent to Jerusalem to rebuild the walls.

## THE MIDNIGHT RIDE OF NEHEMIAH

In 1860, Henry Wadsworth Longfellow composed his famous poem, "The Midnight Ride of Paul Revere." My father, Pastor Arnold Schlueter, who just turned eighty-six years old, can still quote the poem that he learned years ago as a youth. The opening lines read:

"Listen my children and you shall hear
Of the midnight ride of Paul Revere,
On the eighteenth of April, in Seventy-five;
Hardly a man is now alive
Who remembers that famous day and year.
He said to his friend, "If the British march
By land or sea from the town to-night,
Hang a lantern aloft in the belfry arch
Of the North Church tower as a signal light, --
One if by land, and two if by sea;
And I on the opposite shore will be,
Ready to ride and spread the alarm
Through every Middlesex village and farm,
For the country folk to be up and to arm." [21]

Listen my children and you shall hear of the midnight ride of Nehemiah. Six verses (Nehemiah 2:11-16) reveal a very critical strategy that God had released into Nehemiah's heart. Nehemiah arrived in Jerusalem escorted by the horsemen of King Artaxerxes. As the story unfolded Nehemiah carried out a God-given strategy of riding around the destroyed walls and gates of Jerusalem. It is interesting to note at least four very important points about his journey.

1. **Gatekeepers act covertly.** Nehemiah acted covertly. Except for a few men that he had taken into confidence, Nehemiah told no one what he was doing. He was acting covertly or secretly, but not independently. Most of the prayer walks and reconciliation strategies that the Lord has released into the city of Arlington have been carried out "under the radar." The prophetic acts that I mentioned in Chapter Two at Bird's Fort, Village Creek and the headwaters of the Trinity River involved several people, yet they were not widely broadcast prior to or immediately following the acts. They were considered covert in the sense that they were obediently done without fanfare. The deep sensing in my heart is that God will more readily use the behind-the-scenes obedient acts than the out-in-the-open events that are human-driven attempts to fill stadiums, promote ministry and demonstrate unity. I passionately believe that God will bring into our city and region the large stadium gatherings of people who have been or are being transformed by the power of the Lord through His Spirit. However, I also believe – and evidence from other transformed cities and regions supports this belief – that it will happen as a result of the small, passionate, persistent, covert and obedient acts which have flowed from a meeting with God face to face and heart to heart in prayer and worship.

2. **Gatekeepers do not move alone.** Nehemiah did not move alone. The one thing I have learned in the prophetic act of city-reaching and transformation is the simple principle of "you don't move out alone." Nehemiah was secretive about the process of journeying around and surveying the broken walls of the city, but he took others into his confidence. In other words, he did not venture into this project as a lone ranger. This is a very basic Biblical principle we can never forget. Listen to the counsel of God's Word:

"Though one may be overpowered by another, two can withstand
him.
And a threefold cord is not quickly broken" (Ecclesiastes 4:12).

"Where there is no counsel, the people fall;
But in the multitude of counselors there is safety" (Proverbs 11:14).

Again, I say to you that if two of you agree on earth concerning anything that they ask, it will be done for them by My Father in heaven. For where two or three are gathered together in My name, I am there in the midst of them" (Matthew 18:19-20).

Each of us must have a personal and intimate relationship with Jesus Christ. That personal relationship will be strengthened and secured when others come alongside to encourage and support their brother or sister. I can minister as a pastor to my congregation and seek to release life and strength into them through prayer, preaching, teaching and counsel alone or I can call on the elders or ministers that the Lord has lifted up beside me to do the work as a team. The same is true at all levels.

In the realm of spiritual transformation and warfare at a city level, we must work together as the body of Christ. We can seek God with own heart. We can pray alone to receive His strategies. We can have personal time with the King. **But when it comes to taking a city, we have to stretch our arms out and enlist the Church of the city.** One congregation, large or small, cannot do it alone. A truth the Lord released into my heart several years ago was this: He can do more with ten people from ten congregations than He can with fifty people from one congregation. It has to be a family experience. Over the 19 years that I have lived in Arlington, I have witnessed the demise of at least five congregations. Each one of those congregations moved out in great faith and power to conquer evil strongholds in, around and over the city, and all of those congregations are now gone. Do not misunderstand me; I am not giving credence to the fact that the enemy is more powerful than the church. I am acknowledging the fact that our attitudes and acts can never be "We can do this ourselves." We have to find others who will go beside us, move with us, test us, check us out, give us counsel and join us in releasing God's kingdom on earth.

The mustard seed parable in the Gospel of Luke uses the second person plural pronoun "you" when talking to the disciples. In other words, it is the "corporate you" that will tell the mulberry tree to be "pulled up by the roots and be planted in the sea" (Luke 17:6). It will be the corporate bride of Christ that will lead the city into transformation.

Let's examine a bit more the difference between individual and corporate. I believe it can also be called independence and dependence. Many Americans fail to understand or embrace dependence because of our strong heritage as an independent nation. We may be an independent nation and people, but we are still "under God." Independency states "I'm going to do this all by myself" or "I've got the plan. I know what to do and I'm going after this" or "I don't care what the rest of the people, the rest of the church, the rest of my family, or the rest of the city thinks, I'm going to do this on my own." That's independence. Dependence is "I'm going to depend on God, on the church, and on other people" and as I do – authority is released into and through my life."[22]

3. **Gatekeepers wait for God.** Nehemiah waited three days. This seems to be just a simple note added to the text, but again we must ponder its significance. Nehemiah did not rush out to do something. He waited three days before setting out on the strategy the Lord had given him. He had already prayed and fasted for months before he received the strategy but Nehemiah was still willing to wait on the Lord. In personal conversations with pastors from Uganda where some significant transformation has taken place, they were quick to say that the change did not happen overnight. We want something now, but in the matter of transformation – moving out of chaos into order – we must

be willing to passionately seek God's face for strategy, timing and location even if it means we won't see transformation in our generation.

I also believe that it was spiritually significant that Nehemiah waited three days. The number three can symbolically represent divine completeness or perfect testimony.[23] The third day represents the bringing forth of life—creation, exodus, and resurrection. In other words, Nehemiah was working in perfect alignment with God—bringing forth life into the city. He did not rush out to do something in his own strength. Although the Lord had already given him a strategy and King Artaxerxes had already delivered the materials, Nehemiah waited for God's timing. On the third day, he began his process.

4. **Gatekeepers have authority.** Nehemiah had authority! And finally, as a combined summary of the already mentioned points, Nehemiah was moving under the authority or covering of King Artaxerxes. His authority was the King's letter. His authority not only flowed from King Artaxerxes, but more importantly it proceeded from Almighty God. Nehemiah was in alignment with the government of God and the government of man. I personally love the story of the Centurion who comes to Jesus. Please take time to prayerfully read it.

Now when Jesus had entered Capernaum, a centurion came to Him, pleading with Him, saying, "Lord, my servant is lying at home paralyzed, dreadfully tormented."

And Jesus said to him, "I will come and heal him."

The centurion answered and said, "Lord, I am not worthy that You should come under my roof. But only speak a word, and my servant will be healed. For I also am a man under authority, having soldiers under me. And I say to this one, 'Go,' and he goes; and to another, 'Come,' and he comes; and to my servant, 'Do this,' and he does it."

When Jesus heard it, He marveled, and said to those who followed, "Assuredly, I say to you, I have not found such great faith, not even in Israel! And I say to you that many will come from east and west, and sit down with Abraham, Isaac, and Jacob in the kingdom of heaven. But the sons of the kingdom will be cast out into outer darkness. There will be weeping and gnashing of teeth."

Then Jesus said to the centurion, "Go your way; and as you have believed, so let it be done for you." And his servant was healed that same hour (Matthew 8:5-13).

The centurion understood the lines of authority. When he ordered his men to march, they marched. And they marched not because they thought about it and deemed it a good idea. They had been trained to march. They had been trained to hear the voice of their commander. And when the order came – they moved confidently and obediently into battle. The centurion knew that if Jesus just spoke the word or command – things would move and his servant would be healed.

Nehemiah also understood authority. He was not working out of his own reasoning, confidence and strength, but as a man under authority. He had allowed God to train his heart to hear and obey. He had also learned the heart of the King and how to be obedient when the King asked him to serve as a cupbearer. And when God and the King gave the order to go and rebuild the walls – he accepted their word and moved obediently in that authority. **No other word was needed**, and no other word – especially the testimony of his enemies – could sway him from his duty.

Authority flows from our relationship with those who lead, govern, protect and cover us, whether it is an employer, parent, pastor, spouse, president or teacher. We need to strengthen those relationships. We need to pray for those in authority over us. We need to recognize the voice of those who speak into our lives. And when they speak – especially God – we need to authoritatively and obediently move into action.

This is season for agreeing with those we can move with to keep the city we have been assigned to. Intercessors do not go out alone to bring down principalities and powers. Apostles need intercessors to tend or pray in the decrees they make over a city. Prophets "see" in vain if they don't have apostles to declare their revelations. We really do need each other.

## NEHEMIAH EXAMINES THE WALLS AND GATES.

So, Nehemiah moved into action. He went out. He examined the wall. He examined the gates. The text reads that he exited through the Valley Gate and proceeded south towards the Refuse Gate. He examined the broken down and burnt walls all the way to the Fountain Gate and King's Pool. The animal he was riding could not pass through the wall and he turned around and went back to the Valley Gate. He did not circle the whole city. He basically journeyed along the southwest to southeast portion of the city and he closely inspected the walls and gates. He examined them.

From the moment Nehemiah heard about the burnt and broken walls (while he was sitting in Susa) to this very moment when he was examining firsthand the condition of the walls, I believe that he was examining something far deeper than walls. I believe he was examining the spiritual condition of the city. Let's make this very personal for a moment. If the Lord has brought us into a "Nehemiah Season," then a lot more is implied than just the physical rebuilding of a city.

The Lord's interest in transformation begins with a careful examination of our lives. We need to invite God to carry out a thorough examination of everything in our lives so that He can bring about a complete change in our lives. The Lord desires to build each one of us up in our full destiny and purpose in Him, but in order to build He has to first knock down or destroy. Judah had developed a very unhealthy attitude regarding God's temple and His presence. The people disregarded His merciful and compassionate rule over their lives. They despised His covenant relationship with them. The result was a nation that sought after other gods and trampled the poor under their feet. God had to destroy Judah in order to rebuild her. The whole nation of Judah had to go into exile.

The Lord uses the same process with a city that he does with a nation. He uses the same methods with a congregation that He does with a city. He applies the same measures to individuals as He does to the whole congregation. God is serious about returning us – individuals, cities and nations – to our intended status in His Kingdom. In my book Return of the Priests, in commenting on Isaiah 61:1-6, I wrote:

"God declared through the prophet Isaiah that He would pour out His Spirit of anointing upon a chosen one – the Messiah. From that anointing would pour forth healing, restoration, sight and freedom. And not only would those who mourned be consoled, but the streets of the city would be repaired, Isaiah declared, and walls would be rebuilt. Those things torn down by the ages of sin, rebellion and bondage would be restored. And notice that right at the center of this Messianic proclamation is the heart of God. "But you shall be named the priests of the LORD, they shall call you the servants of our God."

You will be a kingdom of priests. You will be treasures in the heart of God. And your kingdom will be of authoritative servanthood. You will reign as servants and God's glory will be upon you. Through your author-ity as priests, lives and streets will be rebuilt. God will not be halted in his desire to bring His people into their destiny.

God will rebuild.

God will restore.

God will bring forth life.

God will do it through His appointed priests.

And He declares, as the pages of Scriptures turn, that His Son will be the perfect representation of His call to priesthood. His Son, Jesus, is the Great High Priest."[24]

All transformation begins with the simple, but necessary, examination of our own walls and gates. It starts with an invitation for Jesus to come and examine us with His love. The presence of His goodness and mercy will lead us to repentance. Repentance will take us to the building up of a new life, a new city and a new nation. This is the season of Nehemiah.

## THE PRAYER OF EXAMINATION

Lord, would You examine everything in my life and make sure everything is in its proper place. Please examine my relationships – especially with those who have authority in my life. Please examine my walls and gates.

Lord, I want to see our nation and city become everything that You meant it to be, but it all begins with Your relationship with me. Lord, everything from my personal life to the city gates has to be in line with You. I cannot deal with the city gates if I don't have alignment here – in my heart. So, examine me. Reveal what needs to go and what can stay. Lead me to repentance and the cleansing of my life. Lord, I believe that You want me to be used as a priest, as a Nehemiah, in my world. Begin the work in my heart. I pray in Your holy name. Amen.

# 6

## Gatekeepers: Called to Build

*Then I said to them, "You see the distress that we are in, how Jerusalem lies waste, and its gates are burned with fire. Come and let us build the wall of Jerusalem, that we may no longer be a reproach." And I told them of the hand of my God which had been good upon me, and also of the king's words that he had spoken to me. So, they said, "Let us rise up and build." Then they set their hands to this good work.*

Nehemiah 2:17-18

When I was a child, I spoke as a child, I understood as a child, I thought as a child; but when I became a man, I put away childish things. For now, we see in a mirror, dimly, but then face to face. Now I know in part, but then I shall know just as I also am known" (1 Corinthians 13:11-12). Throughout high school I planned to be an architect. As I was growing up I loved building things. When I was very young I used Tinker Toys, Lincoln Logs and an Erector Set. As a matter of fact, I have a few scars on my face as a result of getting too close to a homemade fan.

When I started at Texas A&M University, my interest changed from architecture to the outdoors. I worked towards a degree in Recreation and Parks, a stepping stone into the National Park Service. My specialty though had not really changed because I was still being trained to build – not buildings or homes, but trails, interpretative devices and printed materials that would help people understand and enjoy the parks.

The Lord called me into the pastoral ministry during my senior year at college. Then I was trained to build up and equip the saints. At that same time my wife and I started our family, and I met face to face the challenge of building something into the next generation. Throughout my life I have been challenged over and over with a need to build.

As a matter of fact, I believe that all of God's people are called to be builders. We are builders of His kingdom. Anointed by God as His priests, we are called to be partakers of His restorative nature.

"And they shall rebuild the old ruins,

They shall raise up the former desolations,

And they shall repair the ruined cities,

The desolations of many generations" (Isaiah 61:4).

We are exhorted to build upon that foundation which has been laid in us in Christ Jesus. We are co-laborers as we work to establish our lives, the lives of others and, yes, even the life of our city or region, in Christ Jesus.

"According to the grace of God which was given to me, as a wise master builder I have laid the foundation, and another builds on it. But let each one take heed how he builds on it. For no other foundation can anyone lay than that which is laid, which is Jesus Christ. Now if anyone builds on this foundation with gold, silver, precious stones, wood, hay, straw, each one's work will become clear; for the Day will declare it, because it will be revealed by fire; and the fire will test each one's work, of what sort it is. If anyone's work which he has built on it endures, he will receive a reward. If anyone's work is burned, he will suffer loss; but he himself will be saved, yet so as through fire" (1 Corinthians 3:10-15).

## BUILDING ON THE FOUNDATION

The Greek word used for "foundation" is "themelios." It literally means that something is being put down as a substructure or foundation. But the root of this word is "tithemi" which is translated with a variety of words in the New Testament including: appoint, commit, conceive, give, kneel down, lay (aside, down, up), make, ordain, purpose, put, set (forth), settle, and sink down.[25]

In other words, this foundation that is being laid is a preconceived act which has been appointed, conceived, purposed and ordained of God to be laid down as a substructure under our lives and under the life of everything in His kingdom. **I believe that God has literally laid down through His creative and proceeding Word a foundation, an appointment or an ordained destiny for each of our lives.** He has spoken and declared His purposes (or His will) over our families, our cities and our nations. He has pre-destined us to be founded in Christ Jesus.

Interestingly, the Hebrew word for "foundation" is similar. "Yacad" means to set or to intensively found or settle. It can also be translated as appoint, establish, lay a foundation, or ordain.[26] The act of building starts with an appointed foundation. God has appointed a foundation for each of our lives, and it is based and centered on an intimate relationship with Jesus Christ.

But that is only the beginning. Now we must build on that foundation, and what we are building is the temple of God (1 Corinthians 3:16, 17). We must deliberately and intentionally lay hold of that which is in Him and, filled with His Spirit, build upon the foundation of Jesus Christ. The Lord has an appointed and pre-conceived purpose or destiny for each of our lives. He has laid the foundation. Now we must build. God has an appointed purpose or destiny for our families, our cities and our nations. We must rise in the power of His Spirit and build. The Lord has an eternal purpose or destiny for His holy city of Jerusalem. He revealed that purpose to the heart of Nehemiah and Nehemiah began to build.

"Then I said to them, "You see the distress that we are in, how Jerusalem lies waste, and its gates are burned with fire. Come and let us build the wall of Jerusalem, that we may no longer be a reproach." And I told them of the hand of my God which had been good upon me, and also of the king's words that he had spoken to me. So, they said, "Let us rise up and build." Then they set their hands to this good work" (Nehemiah 2:17-18).

## NO LONGER A REPROACH

Nehemiah declared his intentions. "Let us build so that we may no longer be a reproach." The wording here is interesting. Nehemiah realized that the present state of the city was shameful. The city was a reproach. It was not the city of God's purpose and destiny. Decades earlier when the first exiles returned to Jerusalem they established an altar. They built the foundation and the walls of a new temple. The foundation of worship and intimacy had been laid, but nothing had been built upon it. Their work ceased. They did not go on to rebuild the city. They were still living in reproach and shame.

The Hebrew word used for "build" is "banah." Nehemiah called the people to build. The word literally means to build, to make, to set up or to repair. If they would build, set up and repair the city Nehemiah told the people of Jerusalem, their reproach will be gone. Interestingly, the word "banah" also means to obtain children.

## OUR HERITAGE OR DESTINY

The Hebrew people conceptualized something greater than a physical building when they used the word "banah." This word includes the idea of flourishing in life. You build up something so your life will flourish. And for those in the Middle East, life flourished when their house was full of children. Life flourishes when it looks to the coming generations. The Hebrew people were very concerned about their heritage. I believe that this is innately true of most cultures. Whatever your background may be, you want your life to go on into the next generation. I don't think that this concept is solely limited to the physical bearing of offspring. It has everything to do with knowing your life is not limited to just "now," but will go beyond yourself.

Earlier I quoted Isaiah 61:4. Ruins will be rebuilt and that which is desolated will be repaired and restored. Why is it so important for it to be rebuilt? We need to read further.

"Strangers shall stand and feed your flocks,
And the sons of the foreigner
Shall be your plowmen and your vinedressers.
But you shall be named the priests of the LORD,
They shall call you the servants of our God.
You shall eat the riches of the Gentiles,
And in their glory, you shall boast.
**Instead of your shame you shall have double honor,**
**And instead of confusion they shall rejoice in their portion.**
**Therefore, in their land they shall possess double;**
**Everlasting joy shall be theirs**" (Isaiah 61:5-7, emphasis mine).

Rebuilding and restoring releases double honor. It replaces confusion with an awareness of your inheritance or portion in life. Shame is removed and is replaced by everlasting joy. It is a joy that will extend throughout the generations. The future will flourish. Shame will replace reproach. We need an inheritance. We need a heritage that will go after us. We need to rebuild.

This whole idea of building the walls of Jerusalem was not just a great plan to make the city look better or to make it more secure. Building was necessary in order to fulfill the God-appointed destiny of the city. Jerusalem and Arlington and your city must be built and repaired, and set up in order to come to the full covenant promise God breathed into the city when it was conceived. Sound familiar? When you were conceived – when you were still in your mother's womb, according to Psalm 139, God proclaimed a destiny for you in Christ Jesus, and He is breathing His life-giving Word into you to "banah" you into your fullness.

I want the Lord to "banah" the city of Arlington, Texas into its fullness. I want to help Him build up the walls of Arlington. I want that to happen in the physical sense. I want the city to look better. But the real result I am after is not just a pretty city. I really desire and I believe God promises that the spiritual heritage of the city goes far beyond "pretty." I want the city emptied of shame and filled with honor. I want the city emptied of fear and filled with love. I want the city emptied of impurity and filled with holiness. I want death to flee and life to come. Then the city will fully come into God's purpose. It's not just about "pretty."

In our study of Arlington on a natural and spiritual level the pastors and intercessors have discovered that the city has been and is a gathering place. When the city was first founded, people would come from miles around to take advantage of mineral waters flowing from a well in the heart of the city. They would also come for shopping or gambling. People still gather here for rest, food, and entertainment. It has become a bedroom community to the larger cities of Fort Worth and Dallas. It is the hub of professional baseball and football in the region. In the natural Arlington is a gathering place. It's a good or pretty city.

But God has also appointed it to be a gathering place for salvation, life, healing, hope and refuge. Just west of the old well is one of the state's largest outreach and mission centers. People come from hundreds of miles to seek refuge, care and restoration. And I want to witness the spiritual heritage of the city as a gathering place to the extent that the city is a place of life, blessing, hope and love in every aspect of its culture. And not just Arlington, but Dallas, Mansfield, Irving, Fort Worth, Duncanville and all the rest of the region. I pray that all things would come into alignment with God's divine purpose and destiny for them.

In the same way, I pray that God's intended purpose for your life will come into its fullness. When that is done, as Nehemiah declares, the reproach and shame will lift off of us. We will receive the double honor of God. God looks at a life or a city that is in rubble, burned down, destroyed and filled with shame, and He says: "If these people will once again catch in their spirit what is on My heart, then I will move in them and empower them to repair and rebuild their city. I will renew hope to their generation and the generations to come. I will break off their reproach and shame. I will lift it from the city."

Listen carefully! The transformation of our city is not about building new things. It is not solely about repairing things that were torn down or in ruins. The importance of building is discovered as we launch the next generation from the same foundation that we have in Jesus. One of the most important tasks in my personal life is to see my children, their spouses and their children standing on the foundational promises and covenant estab lished by the blood of Jesus Christ. That is the heart of their appointed destiny in God.

The same theme was present at Jericho after the people of Israel crossed the Jordan under the leadership of Joshua. At Gilgal—the new generation was circumcised and the reproach of Egypt and the shame of bondage and slavery was removed. And what was their first task in the new land? They were to bring forth or build the destiny of God by tearing down the old walls of Jericho.

Again, this is not just about building new walls. It is
a reestablishment of covenant,
a removal of reproach
and the setting in of a new generation.
It is about people and cities coming into God's purpose.
It is about God releasing heaven on earth
and bringing the nations back into their divine alignment.
It is about the transforming nature of our God
as He moves on each generation throughout all of time.

## RISE UP AND BUILD

The favor of God was on Nehemiah and the people agreed to "rise up and build." They set their hands to the work. The Hebrew word for hand is "yad." It literally means "open hands for strength, consecration, domin-ion, power, fellowship, order and praise."[27] It is the root word in "yadah" which means praise. Praise means to extend holy and consecrated hands to God in worship and adoration. In the extending of the hands there is the release of praise, dominion, strength and order. As people responded to Nehemiah's call, they did so with a renewed consecration unto God and His purposes. They lifted up their hands in the acknowledgement and praise of God – allowing their hands to form mortar, bricks, and walls, not as slaves in either Egypt or Babylon, but as servants, ambassadors and priests of the Most High God. Let us consecrate ourselves unto the Lord. Let us rise up in the power of His Spirit and build!

## THE PRAYER OF RESTORATION

Lord, restore us! Bring us individually and corporately into the full destiny for which we were created. Help us as gatekeepers to build the new walls, to reestablish Your covenant with us, to remove the reproach of our past and help us to look beyond ourselves into the lives of the future generations. We invite Your Holy Spirit to come and to empower us to rise up and build. Let our lives, our families, our churches and our cities come into the fullness of the destiny You have purposed. Begin the work in my heart. I pray in Jesus' name. Amen.

# 7

## The Enemy Within

*But when Sanballat the Horonite, Tobiah the Ammonite official, and Geshem the Arab heard of it, they laughed at us and despised us, and said, "What is this thing that you are doing? Will you rebel against the king?" So, I answered them, and said to them, "The God of heaven Himself will prosper us; therefore, we His servants will arise and build, but you have no heritage or right or memorial in Jerusalem*

(Nehemiah 2:19-20)

### THE ENEMY

Chapter Three of the book of Nehemiah clearly details the rebuilding process of Jerusalem. I wish I could say that the position of gatekeeper is one without trial or heartache but if I did someone would say "liar, liar, pants on fire!" Before restoration could be realized Nehemiah and the returning Jews had to go through the time of transition many of us are facing now. They had to enter that dangerous place that Beverly McIntyre of Change Point Ministries in Arizona calls "the threshold". A later chapter in this book will deal with the threshold in more depth. Consider at this

point her main premise. This is it: We will face our deadliest enemies as we cross over the threshold of the doorway to our destiny. With that in mind, let's look at the last two verses of Chapter Two in Nehemiah.

When we move out into God's promise the enemy will never fail to raise up his ugly head. When he does, we must never forget that…

God has a destiny for us regardless of our background or station in life.

God has heard our cry of repentance.

God has poured His favor and provision into our lives.

God has ordained us as priests to build, repair and restore.

"He who is in us is greater than he who is in the world" (1 John 4:4)! And, as Paul declared, "if God is for us, who can be against us" (Romans 8:31b)? Nothing can overcome us or destroy us as we stand on Jesus Christ.

As we journey through this chapter and others describing Nehemiah's enemies we need to remember Nehemiah's words to his enemies: "The God of heaven Himself will prosper us; therefore, we His servants will arise and build, but you have no heritage or right or memorial in Jerusalem (Nehemiah 2:20).

## THE ENEMY DEFINED

You will recall that Nehemiah's name means "the comfort of God." We're talking here about a comfort released through Nehemiah's act of repentance. We are well aware that Nehemiah's name is very significant in understanding the message of the book of Nehemiah. In the same way, the names and ploys of his enemies are significant. Let's take a look of them.

## SANBALLAT

Sanballat was the satrap or governor of Samaria – the region to the immediate north of Jerusalem and the province of Judah. Sanballat was a Horonite. That places his lineage back to the Moabites who were fierce enemies of Judah and Israel. Since his name is Babylonian in origin, Sanballat was more than likely appointed by the previous Babylonian leadership to watch over the puppet province of Samaria. He then became a Persian satrap who answered to Artaxerxes. The name Sanballat is intriguing. It is a Babylonian name meaning "the Moon god gives life." In Nelson's Bible Dictionary, it reads:

"In papyri found at the Jewish settlement in Elephantine, Egypt, Sanballat is called the governor of Samaria. His daughter married "one of the sons of Joiada, the son of Eliashib the high priest" (Nehemiah 13:28). Nehemiah viewed such a "mixed marriage" as a defilement of the priesthood, so he drove Joiada away. Sanballat's opposition to Nehemiah's work may have stemmed from jealousy. He may have felt that his authority was threatened by the reawakening of the land of Judah. After mocking Nehemiah and his crew, he tried to slip through the broken wall of Jerusalem with people from other enemy nations to kill the Jews. Nehemiah thwarted this plot, setting up guards of half the people while the other half worked (Nehemiah 4:7-23). Neither did he fall for Sanballat's ploy to come outside the wall for a "friendly" discussion (Nehemiah 6:3)."[28]

Sanballat saw everything that Nehemiah was doing as rebellion against the king and against his god. Sanballat served a foreign king and a foreign God – a religious system that greatly opposed the establishment of God's kingdom and purpose in Jerusalem.

## TOBIAH

The old gangster movies portrayed the tough mob boss surrounded by a bunch of men who did whatever they were ordered. Tobiah seemed to be nothing more than Sanballat's "yes" man. His name is actually Hebrew in origin and means "the goodness of God," but he was called an Ammonite (another ancient foe of Israel located to the east of Judah). Some records seem to show that Tobiah was originally from Judah, but was part of the families that deserted their homeland and people to escape the Babylonian occupation. Nehemiah is harsh towards the Ammonites as he chides the people of Judah for their intermarriage with pagans.

In those days, I also saw Jews who had married women of Ashdod, **Ammon**, and Moab. And half of their children spoke the language of Ashdod, and could not speak the language of Judah, but spoke according to the language of one or the other people. So, I contended with them and cursed them, struck some of them and pulled out their hair, and made them swear by God, saying, "You shall not give your daughters as wives to their sons, nor take their daughters for your sons or yourselves. Did not Solomon king of Israel sin by these things? Yet among many nations there was no king like him, who was beloved of his God; and God made him king over all Israel. Nevertheless, pagan women caused even him to sin. Should we then hear of your doing all this great evil, transgressing against our God by marrying pagan women" (Nehemiah 13:23-27, emphasis mine)?

Notice that Tobiah's ancestors had fled to **Ammon** and now he returned to Samaria as nothing more than a "yes" man, a pagan, to one of Judah's deadliest foes. His name, "the goodness of God", was in direct contradiction to the path he chose to walk.

## GESHEM

Geshem, the Arab, is identified as a powerful tribal chieftain from the Persian province of Arabia. The Wycliffe Bible Commentary assigns him as the probable "governor of Dedan or the chief of some Arab tribe living south of Jerusalem."[29] His name literally means "rain" or "shower." Not much is said about him but it is interesting to note that although his name as Sanballat's and Tobiah's had positive connotations – life, goodness and rain - each of these unholy men decided to act in the opposite spirit or destiny of their names. They were surely influenced by the false gods they served.

The spiritual forces that drove these three men in their plots to destroy the re-building of Jerusalem are still in force. They desire to destroy any attempt of bringing forth God's kingdom and will on earth as it in heaven.

## OUR ANCIENT FOE

These enemies of Nehemiah worshipped false gods. As a matter of record, the reason both Israel (the Northern Kingdom) and Judah (the Southern Kingdom) had both fallen captive to the Assyrians and Babylonians respectively was the deliberate act of worshipping false gods. Hosea declared that Israel had married Baal – the ancient god of fertility. This was the same principality that Abraham, Isaac, Gideon and David had all contented with. Jeremiah declared:

"For the LORD of hosts, who planted you, has pronounced doom against you for the evil of the house of Israel and of the house of Judah, which they have done against themselves to provoke Me to anger in offering incense to Baal" (Jeremiah 11:17).

The people had forsaken their true husband – the Lord God Almighty – to pursue Baal. Things have not changed much. Early in the summer of 2006, my wife, Kay, and I were members of a strategic prayer team that went to Pampa, Texas. Pampa is located in the upper panhandle of Texas. All of Texas had been under a severe drought, and it was intensely apparent in West Texas. Tens of thousands of cattle and other livestock had perished in the dry, barren land scorched by wildfires. Hundreds of thousands of acres had burned. We joined other key intercessory leaders from the State of Texas as well as Apostle Jay Swallow of the Cheyenne Nation in Oklahoma. The fertility of the land was decimated. We journeyed to key areas of the region that had been affected by broken covenants, the shedding of innocent blood and the decimation of the buffalo herds – an act intended to destroy the habitat of the Native Americans. We sought the face of the Lord. We moved obediently towards repentance, reconciliation and healing. As we ended our assignment, rain started falling on Pampa, and a beautiful double rainbow stretched across the sky. Since then there have been numerous drought-breaking rains in the region. The tall lush pampas grass that gave the area its name is growing again. God is healing the land.

During the meetings in Pampa, Apostle Jay Swallow pointed out the key which unlocked the true problem. Something had been discovered a few years earlier in the region. Within 100 miles north of Pampa in the panhandle of Oklahoma, there were a series of caves discovered that contained drawings and inscriptions of the ancient inhabitants of the region.[30] After a thorough investigation the drawings were classified, not as ancient drawings of the Native Americans, but as drawings of Egyptian influence. There were drawings depicting Anubis – the Egyptian god (jackal–like petroglyph) of the dead, Baal the Sun god standing on a throne, and an occultic solar calendar with its accompanying wall pointer which determined the day when Baal (the god of fertility) was to be worshipped. These ancient drawings which preceded the time of the Comanche, Cheyenne and other First Nations people were used to dedicate the land (and we are talking here about America) to Baal. There is nothing new under the heavens! In January of 2007, Dutch Sheets at the "Starting the Year Off Right" conference in Denton, Texas made a clear declaration that Baal is the chief principality or strongman over our nation and we must prepare our hearts and weapons to dismantle this ancient foe in the power of the Lord.

All of this goes to show that things don't change much in the enemy's camp! Martin Luther in his great hymn "A Mighty Fortress is Our God" declared the truth about "our ancient foe." The foe that faced Nehemiah is the same enemy that faces us in our 'modern' spiritual warfare. The ancient foe that faced Adam and Eve is the same one that seeks the downfall of your destiny and the destiny of your city. Satan and his minions are the ancient foe. And the ploys used by the enemy remain similar. We need to discern the enemy but not focus on him. We need to understand his tactics but we need to move in the strategies of our King – the Lord Jesus Christ. He is our ancient foe but the name of Jesus will bring him down. As Nehemiah did, we must make clear our testimony that we will not worship, marry or make covenant with false gods. We must stand steadfast and immovable in the Lord as the enemy wields his schemes.

In the Book of Nehemiah, the enemy's schemes, primarily fueled by the Baal structure, were enacted through Sanballat, Tobiah and Geshem. They laughed at, loathed and challenged Nehemiah. They laughed at Nehemiah's attempts to rebuild a wall around the city. They saw this act of rebuilding as mere foolishness. They laughed in the same way as those who observed Noah and his sons and made fun of what they labeled a silly project!

They despised Nehemiah as Eliab despised his brother David in 1 Samuel 17. David had heard the challenges of Goliath and responded in faith.

Then David spoke to the men who stood by him, saying, "What shall be done for the man who kills this Philistine and takes away the reproach from Israel? For who is this uncircumcised Philistine, that he should defy the armies of the living God?" And the people answered him in this manner, saying, "So shall it be done for the man who kills him." Now Eliab his oldest brother heard when he spoke to the men; and Eliab's anger was aroused against David, and he said, "Why did you come down here? And with whom have you left those few sheep in the wilderness? I know your pride and the insolence of your heart, for you have come down to see the battle" (1 Samuel 17:26-28).

Eliab loathed David. He saw his confidence as pride and arrogance. He ridiculed his younger brother out of fear and shame. He did not want to be upstaged by his younger brother. In a similar way, Nehemiah represented a serious threat to Sanballat's authority in the region. Out of fear, anger and resentment, the unholy trio acted out their hatred.

The enemies of Nehemiah went beyond laughing. They began to challenge him openly. We will examine this challenge in Chapters Twelve and Thirteen but let's take a moment to read it now.

But it so happened, when Sanballat heard that we were rebuilding the wall, that he was furious and very indignant, and mocked the Jews. And he spoke before his brethren and the army of Samaria, and said, "What are these feeble Jews doing? Will they fortify themselves? Will they offer sacrifices? Will they complete it in a day? Will they revive the stones from the heaps of rubbish -- stones that are burned?" Now Tobiah the Ammonite was beside him, and he said, "Whatever they build, if even a fox goes up on it, he will break down their stone wall" (Nehemiah 4:1-3).

Earlier we discovered that Sanballat and Geshem were local governors placed in authority by the Persian government. We need to re-visit some earlier verses in Nehemiah.

Then I went to the governors in the region beyond the River, and gave them the king's letters. Now the king had sent captains of the army and horsemen with me. When Sanballat the Horonite and Tobiah the Ammonite official heard of it, they were deeply disturbed that a man had come to seek the well-being of the children of Israel" (Nehemiah 2:9-10).

When Nehemiah first arrived in Judah he delivered the official documents from Artaxerxes to Sanballat and Tobiah. They had seen with their own eyes that Artaxerxes had officially blessed and provided for the restoration of Jerusalem under Nehemiah's leadership. And they now have the gall and audacity to say, "What are you doing and why are you rebelling against the king?" Nehemiah, as we mentioned in Chapter Five, was acting according to the authority of God and King Artaxerxes. Sanballat and Tobiah were challenging that authority. They were challenging the very edict of their own king. Sound familiar?

Now the serpent was more cunning than any beast of the field which the LORD God had made. And he said to the woman, "Has God indeed said, 'You shall not eat of every tree of the garden'?" And the woman said to the serpent, "We may eat the fruit of the trees of the garden; but of the fruit of the tree which is in the midst of the garden, God has said, 'You shall not eat it, nor shall you touch it, lest you die.'" Then the serpent said to the woman, "You will not surely die. For God knows that in the day you eat of it your eyes will be opened, and you will be like God, knowing good and evil" (Genesis 3:1-5).

## NEHEMIAH'S ANSWER

Adam and Eve gave up their authority. They chose to be like gods (choosing their own destiny) rather than being in the image of Almighty God (living a fruitful destiny full of life, revelation and authority). Nehemiah chose the latter and declared:

The God of heaven Himself will prosper us; therefore, we His servants will arise and build, but you have no heritage or right or memorial in Jerusalem (Nehemiah 2:20).

Nehemiah did not flinch. He did not waste his time in endless arguments and reasoning. He did not try to compromise. He did not do that which would have been 'politically correct' or advantageous. He turned his eyes on God and declared that this ancient foe had no right, heritage or memorial in the place and plans of the Ancient of Days. God had laid out a plan in Nehemiah's heart and he would not forsake it.

God has a plan and destiny for your life and the life of your church, neighborhood, city and nation. He has a part for you to play in rebuilding, restoration and renewal. God is bringing forth His kingdom through us who believe. In closing out this chapter, let us spend a moment in prayer.

LET US PRAY.

Father God, come and examine my life and everything in it. Examine my workplace. Examine my family. Examine my city. Examine my heart! Examine it with Your holy Word and by Your Holy Spirit. Show me Lord how you want to restore and rebuild my life, city and nation by Your power and Your strength. Grant me Your decrees of favor, provision, power and faith to carry it out for Your glory. And Lord, let it be known from this day forth that the enemy, Satan himself and all of his spirits, have no heritage here. He has no heritage in my family. He has no right in my workplace. He has no memorial in my school and my city. He has no place in my heart. Thank you, Lord God. You are the mighty one. You are the famous one. You are the Ancient of Days. I give you praise in Jesus' name. Amen

# 8

# It's all About the Gates

*Then Eliashib the high priest rose up with his brethren the priests and built the Sheep Gate; they consecrated it and hung its doors. They built as far as the Tower of the Hundred, and consecrated it, then as far as the Tower of Hananel. Next to Eliashib the men of Jericho built. And next to them Zaccur the son of Imri built*

(NEHEMIAH 3:1-3).

## LET'S REVIEW

 In the darkest times—God brought forth faith, life and comfort. Out of the darkness of God (Hachaliah) came forth the comfort of God (Nehemiah). God used a cupbearer who responded to the news about Jerusalem with prayer and fasting. Nehemiah, the cupbearer received favor before the king and was sent to Jerusalem to rebuild her walls. Nehemiah was working in perfect alignment with God.

Nehemiah did not move alone. His authority was the King's own decree—not the permission of the Jews, priests, nobles, officials, or others. Nehemiah examined the walls and gates. He declared his intentions – let us build that we may no longer be a reproach. Let us restore, under the mighty hand of God, the inheritance, covenant promises and destiny that God has for us and all succeeding generations. And remember that the enemy has no heritage in our midst.

## REBUILDING THE WALLS

The message of Nehemiah is usually focused on the walls that Nehemiah was called to rebuild, but somewhere in the midst of my meditations, research and readings of Nehemiah, I began to see a fresh revelation from the Lord. The work that Nehemiah did was not about the walls. It was about the gates. As I read the chapters in Nehemiah regarding the rebuilding of the walls, I saw a noticeable concentration on the gates. Everything is highlighted around the gates. Notice that in the first few verses of Nehemiah chapter three the first thing constructed was the Sheep Gate by the priest Eliashib and his brother priests. They constructed it. They consecrated it. They hung its doors. Then they started building the wall next to it. The gate was the first part of the wall reconstructed and it was accomplished by the priests.

The sons of Hassenaah built the Fish Gate. They laid its beams and hung its doors with bolts and bars. They then built the wall next to it. The story continues. "Moreover, Jehoiada the son of Paseah and Meshullam the son of Besodeiah repaired the Old Gate; they laid its beams and hung its doors, with its bolts and bars" (Nehemiah 3:6-7). The same is true of the Refuse Gate, the Valley Gate and the Fountain Gate.

Does it strike you odd that in Nehemiah's report the gates were built before the walls? How many times have you gone by a construction site and noticed gates standing by themselves with no walls? Usually the walls are built first, and an opening is left to be later filled in with a door or a gate. But this is not the case in Nehemiah. The gate was central to the story. The gate was constructed, consecrated and completed before work even started on the walls. I very strongly believe that it was God Himself who spoke this building method into Nehemiah's heart. I am not sure if this was a common practice or not of the builders in the time of Nehemiah. Of one thing, I am sure – there was obviously a focus placed on the construction of the gates.

Let me take you back a moment to an earlier part of Israel's history. At Mt. Carmel, Elijah confronted the false prophets of Baal. When the efforts of the false prophets failed to bring forth a fire to their altar, it was Elijah's turn. Elijah built an altar, but his own words show that he did it according to God's specific counsel:

And it came to pass, at the time of the offering of the evening sacrifice, that Elijah the prophet came near and said, "LORD God of Abraham, Isaac, and Israel, let it be known this day that You are God in Israel and I am Your servant, and that I have done all these things at Your word" (1 Kings 18:36).

Paul Keith Davis in his book, Thrones of Our Soul, writes about Elijah:

"He first restored the altar of God that had been destroyed during the times of apostasy and then gathered twelve stones to represent God's governmental arrangement. He followed up by pouring water on an altar that was to be consumed with fire – the opposite of what the natural mind would suggest. Nonetheless, **he performed each task by the Lord's counsel**…Upon completion; Elijah declared he had done all those things by the Lord's instruction. Therefore, when he called upon the Lord for the demonstration of His power, the spirit of might was present to accompany the spirit of counsel released to Elijah in the preparation of the altar. The spirit of might supported and affirmed the careful obedience to the spirit of counsel followed by the prophet"[31] (emphasis mine).

In other words, Elijah was obedient to the details of God's counsel and therefore God released His might or power upon the altar. In like manner, God delivered to Nehemiah the divine order for rebuilding the walls even though it seemed contrary to the natural way of building. Nehemiah was obedient to God's plan so God released His power, purpose into Jerusalem.

So, what is God's plan? What is important about the gates? What do the gates represent in God's heart that He desired to release into the structure of a rebuilt Jerusalem? What does this have to do with us?

THE GATES ARE CALLED "PRAISE."
But you shall call your walls Salvation,
  And your gates Praise (Isaiah 60:18b).

Enter into His gates with thanksgiving,
And into His courts with praise.
Be thankful to Him, and bless His name.
For the LORD is good;
His mercy is everlasting,
And His truth endures to all generations (Psalm 100:4-5).

The gates are called "Praise." The gates here are more than just a mere representation of praise – they are praise. The key that will unlock the destiny of Jerusalem will be praise. The door or gate which opens into Jerusalem's future purpose will be identified and released with worship. The gates were built first because praise is at the head of the processional. Life is released when we praise the Creator and Giver of Life. Praise gains the victory (1 Chronicles 20:1-30). Praise establishes God's throne (Psalm 22:3). Praise destroys heaviness of spirit (Isaiah 61:3). The walls of salvation – both for Jerusalem and for each of us – will be built around our intimate and worshipful relationship with God.

I would like for you to imagine something for a moment. You are standing in the middle of a room. Surrounding you are the walls of salvation. In other words, in Christ you are completely engulfed in the presence of God. You are planted and standing on His grace. He is surrounding you with His love, salvation and mercy. He is covering every aspect of your life with His holy and precious blood. He is covering you with His righteousness. Now look around and locate the doors to the room. Imagine every door is labeled "Praise." Nothing can come in or go out unless it is filtered by and through your praises unto God.

Can you imagine what your life would be like if all your thoughts and actions were governed by praise and thanksgiving? Your life would come into alignment with God's heart. God would be enthroned over you. He would release life, victory and purpose in and through you. You would be a vehicle – an instrument – of His praise, salvation and kingdom in the earth.

When God commanded Nehemiah to start with the gates in rebuilding the walls of Jerusalem, He was declaring that Jerusalem was to be a vehicle or instrument of God's praise –a praise in the earth.

I have set watchmen on your walls, O Jerusalem;

They shall never hold their peace day or night.
You who make mention of the LORD, do not keep silent,
And give Him no rest till He establishes
And till He makes Jerusalem a praise in the earth (Isaiah 62:6-7)

God wants Jerusalem to be a praise in the earth. He wants your life to be a praise in the earth. He also wants your home and your city to be a praise in the earth. God establishes His presence as king (Psalm 22:3) upon the praises of His people. He enters in with authority through these gates labeled praise. But there is another name given to the gates.

## THE GATES ARE CALLED "RIGHTEOUSNESS."

Open to me the gates of righteousness;
 I will go through them,
 And I will praise the LORD.
 This is the gate of the LORD,
 Through which the righteous shall enter (Psalm 118:19-20).

The gates are called "Praise." They are also called "Righteousness." Let me repeat what I asked earlier. Can you imagine what your life would be like if all your thoughts and actions were governed by praise and thanksgiving? **Your life would come into alignment with God's heart.** That is a simple definition of righteousness. The righteous person's life is lined up rightly with God.

Before we go on I think it is very important for us to grasp the simplicity of the word "righteousness." In Hebrew, the word righteousness means right or just. In Greek, the foundation of the word implies equity. To be righteous is to do that which is right or just (equitable). Your life is meant to be balanced (like the scales of justice) and cleansed (not filled with that which is wrong). Without God, we can journey towards righteousness on our own but we will always fall short. We cannot do that which is right and just because our lives are out of alignment or sync with God (we are sinners). In both the Old and New Testaments righteousness is released into our lives as we turn to God in faith. Regarding Abram, it is written: "And he believed in the LORD, and He accounted it to him for righteousness" (Genesis 15:6). Paul, in writing to the Romans, refers back to Abraham and declares: "For what does the Scripture say? 'Abraham believed God, and it was accounted to him for righteousness.' Now to him who works, the wages are not counted as grace but as debt. But to him who does not work but believes on Him who justifies the ungodly, his faith is accounted for righteousness, just as David also describes the blessedness of the man to whom God imputes righteousness apart from works" (Romans 4:3-6).

In simple terms, when we set the eyes of our heart on the Lord our life becomes righteous, just, cleansed and balanced. When we believe in Him, He imparts or imputes to us His righteousness. When we praise Him He enthrones Himself in our midst.

The walls around Jerusalem are called salvation. The gates are called praise and righteousness. God's plan was and is that everyone going in and out of Jerusalem would have their lives filled with praise (hearts of faith directed to God) and would be righteous (their lives filled with God). These are the gates that we are commanded, like Nehemiah, to build.

Now read carefully! As we build the gates, God's praise and righteousness is being established and released – not only in Jerusalem but throughout the earth! He is enlisting us to extend His kingdom throughout the earth. He has extended His royal scepter to us and has given us authority to establish His praise and righteousness. Jerusalem represents the throne room of God. Nothing can enter the throne room of God's presence except through the praise and righteousness which is secured through the work of Jesus Christ. God has secured a gate into His presence through His Son.

Therefore, brethren, having boldness to enter the Holiest by the blood of Jesus, by a new and living way which He consecrated for us, through the veil, that is, His flesh, and having a High Priest over the house of God, let us draw near with a true heart in full assurance of faith, having our hearts sprinkled from an evil conscience and our bodies washed with pure water. Let us hold fast the confession of our hope without wavering, for He who promised is faithful (Hebrews 10:19-23).

Jesus is the gate into the presence of the Father. God has declared that all those who enter into His presence must come through the true and only gate (door) of His Son Jesus Christ. Jesus is the most righteous One.

And God has appointed us as gates to release the Father's kingdom into the world. **This is an important and key point that we will delve into more in coming chapters.** Let us draw near to Him with a true heart. Let us hold fast the confession of our hope. Let us as gates release His kingdom to the ends of earth.

As we close this chapter, let me challenge you to invite the Lord to reveal His heart to you regarding those gates. For as we look at the gates of Jerusalem, so the Lord wants to establish those same gates in your city, your state and your nation. God wants to be enthroned – not only in Jerusalem – but wherever you live.

Lift up your heads, O you gates!
And be lifted up, you everlasting doors!
And the King of glory shall come in.
Who is this King of glory?
The LORD strong and mighty,
The LORD mighty in battle.
Lift up your heads, O you gates!
Lift up, you everlasting doors!
And the King of glory shall come in.
Who is this King of glory?
The LORD of hosts,
He is the King of glory (Psalm 24:7-10).

And if Jesus is the true Gate of Righteousness and we are in Him and He is in us – then we are gates and gatekeepers.

LET US PRAY.

For our prayer let us make simple declaration of faith. Lord, I turn the eyes of my heart to You. You are my salvation. You are my righteousness. I praise You. You are the gate into the Father's presence and I boldly come through You. Lord, I commit myself to You as a gate. Lord – establish Your gates here – where I live. Let those gates be established in praise and righteousness. Let those gates be opened to the King of glory. Let Your kingdom come into all the earth. Let Your good pleasure be established to the ends of the earth!

# 9

# The Purpose Of Gates

*"This is why there is a Church, the body of Christ. We make God legal in the earth. How does it happen that God needs legal entry to that which He created? He gave the earth to Adam. Adam sold it in sin to the Devil."*

DR. RONALD E. COTTLE, *STUDIES IN NEHEMIAH*[32]

## THE GATES ARE IMPORTANT

In December of 2000 I attended the first annual International Coalition of Apostles (ICA) meeting. The overseeing apostle is Dr. C. Peter Wagner. The primary purpose of ICA is to gather apostles and apostolic ministries from around the world to report on and discuss what God is doing in the world. It is not a decision-making group, but a place of discussion, prayer, fellowship and connections. The first meeting was held in Arlington, Texas. At that initial meeting, one of the first persons I met was Dr. Ron Cottle, the founder and president of Beacon University in Georgia. He gave me a signed copy of one of his books – Studies in Nehemiah. It languished on my book shelf until four years later when I opened it to read these words by Dr. Cottle:

"We should begin with the understanding that the main purpose of the builders in Jerusalem was to build gates, not walls."[33]

I shared in the last chapter that there is a definite concentration on the gates in the book of Nehemiah. Everything is centered on them. The gates were put into position and then the walls were reconstructed. Therefore, it is extremely important to focus our attention on the gates. What do they represent? How do they fit into God's scheme of things?

We can summarize an examination of the gates and what they represent in these few statements:

- Gates control access into and out of the city.
- Gates represent the heart of government and authority.
- Gates represent commerce and business.

## GATES CONTROL ACCESS.

The gates of a city control access in and out of the city. Obviously, this is one of the primary functions of a gate. When a door or gate is closed, no one can come in. When you open it, people may enter. The Hebrew word for gate is "sha'ar." It simply means "an opening, such as a door or gate."[34]

A door or a gate in a city, a business, a church or a home is an entry point, a point of access into that city or home. It is extremely important to guard, watch and judge places of access in order to control what comes in and what goes out. We will examine the word "sha'ar" closer in a moment.

## GATES REPRESENT GOVERNMENT AND AUTHORITY.

Gates represent the heart of government and authority. In ancient times, it was at the gates, not at city hall, the jail or the courthouse, that justice was reached and meted out. Our systems of governmental authority have transitioned into buildings, but in Biblical times the heart of governmental authority was at the gate.

"If a man has a stubborn and rebellious son who will not obey the voice of his father or the voice of his mother, and who, when they have chastened him, will not heed them, then his father and his mother shall take hold of him and bring him out to **the elders of his city, to the gate of his city.** And they shall say to the elders of his city, 'This son of ours is stubborn and rebellious; he will not obey our voice; he is a glutton and a drunkard.' Then all the men of his city shall stone him to death with stones; so, you shall put away the evil from among you, and all Israel shall hear and fear" (Deuteronomy 21:18-21, emphasis mine).

Interesting! That text can give us serious food for thought as we deal with our rebellious children. But we can't go there right now. In the spring of 2003 I lead a prayer journey to Israel. On that trip, we visited the ancient city of Dan, which is located in the foothills south of Mount Hermon. During that visit, we walked through the old streets of the city and came to the gate of Dan. Our guide told us that it was at the gate that the king actually sat to issue his proclamations of judgment and authority.

In a similar visit to the ruins of Megiddo we could easily identify the area of the gate where the city elders would sit and determine justice. At the gate, the elders could monitor who was entering or the exiting the city. As individuals or groups came into the city, they literally came under the authority and justice of those sitting at the gates. To sit at the gates was a sign that you had control or authority over those gates. Notice what God declared to Abraham after his testing with Isaac.

"By Myself I have sworn," says the LORD, "because you have done this thing, and have not withheld your son, your only son – blessing I will bless you, and multiplying I will multiply your descendants as the stars of the heaven and as the sand which is on the seashore; and your descendants shall **possess the gate of their enemies**" (Genesis 22:16, 17, emphasis mine).

## GATES REPRESENT COMMERCE AND BUSINESS.

Thus, says the LORD: "Take heed to yourselves, and bear no burden on the Sabbath day, nor bring it in by the gates of Jerusalem; nor carry a burden out of your houses on the Sabbath day, nor do any work, but hallow the Sabbath day, as I commanded your fathers" (Jeremiah 17:21-22).

The gates also represented commerce and business. This is the image we usually see when we think of the gates of a city – people entering the city with their livelihood – their carts, horses, camels and donkeys. There is a tremendous amount of activity at the gate as people come and go buying and selling their wares.

We still see that ancient image of gates in action today. I have journeyed to Texas A&M University, my alma mater, to attend football games with my son and daughter-in-law. Outside the gates of the stadium at booths and stands people were selling food, souvenirs and clothing. There were "on-site" radio stations. There were families and friends huddled around grills. And, if you looked closely you could see police officers and other officials watching the proceedings at the gates – where the action is!

In Nehemiah's time, the elders or the judges at the gates were charged to make sure that the commerce and business that was coming into the city was acceptable. They also judged what was going out. The city gate was the heart of commerce. Even though there might be business centers and shops within the city and places and people of commerce outside the city, it was at the gate that all commerce and business was judged.

As a point of reference, our modern gates are the highways, streets, railways, ports (air and sea) and rivers that enter and exit a city or a region. Our present-day gates are the doors into our businesses, city halls, schools and churches. Our modern portals are televisions, radios, cell phones, internet modems, fiber optic cables and other sophisticated devices which allow access through the airwaves of our lives. Our personal doors are the five senses of sight, smell, taste, touch and hearing that allow access of exterior influences (good or evil) into our heart. It is extremely important that we understand the purpose of these portals and guard the access to our lives through our gates.

And as I stated in the last chapter, if Jesus is the true Gate of Righteousness and we are in Him and He is in us – then we also are gates and gatekeepers. God is positioning us to guard and judge all points of access into our lives, therefore we need to examine God's plan for the gates and gatekeepers. We will study gatekeepers in the next chapter. Let's look now at His plan for gates.

## GOD'S PERFECT PLAN FOR GATES

As mentioned earlier, the Hebrew word used for "gate" is extremely important. The word "sha'ar" obviously means a gate, door or portal. But the word "sha'ar" actually has a root word in it which it is spelled the same way, but pronounced with different inflection. The root word means "to split or to open."[35] So the word is not only referring to the actual opening which is called a door or gate, but also to that which passes through, splits through, or pierces through that opening. It is that which passes through the door that is extremely important for us to understand.

If God has put a gate, a door or a portal in place, the key question is what does the Lord want to pass through the gate? And if you and I are the gates, what does the Lord want to pass through you and me? What does the Lord want to release through your life and mine? What needs to be imparted to us and through us into our immediate surroundings and into the world that we live in?

Dr. Cottle begins our answer by writing, "The concept behind "sha'ar" is piercing the darkness. The visual concept is opening the gate so that the light can shine through and pierce (the darkness). This is what a gate is. The gate of revelation dispels ignorance and opens the door to the mind of God; the gate of faith dispels doubt and opens the door to the miracles of God; the gate of love dispels prejudice and opens the door to the mercy of God."[36]

We have already discovered that the Lord calls the gates of the city "Praise" (Isaiah 60:18) and "Righteousness" (Psalm 118:19). He wants worship and praise to go through us, and He desires His goodness to be evident in us. As we represent the gates of our homes, our workplaces and our cities, the praise and righteousness of God will go through us and will allow the presence of God to be introduced into every place and situation.

Let's go deeper. Look at Genesis 3:22-24: "Then the LORD God said, 'Behold, the man has become like one of Us, to know good and evil. And now, lest he put out his hand and take also of the tree of life, and eat, and live forever'—therefore the LORD God sent him out of the garden of Eden to till the ground from which he was taken. So, He drove out the man; and He placed cherubim at the east of the garden of Eden, and a flaming sword which turned every way, to guard the way to the tree of life." This passage is obviously dealing with the fall of Adam and Eve. But before we look at the fall, let's review what Adam and Eve had been given. In my book Return of the Priests I write:

"...God clearly gave marching orders to Adam. He was commanded to be fruitful or to cause fruit to come forth. He was to multiply – to increase. He was ordered to fill or replenish the earth and have dominion over it. God was giving Adam authority over all of creation. It would be Adam's responsibility to care for creation. What an awesome privilege! What an overwhelming responsibility! Authority and reign were given to Adam and Eve, but this responsibility was meant to be woven together with intimacy with the Creator."[37]

God had entrusted all dominion to Adam and Eve. He had given them the authority to keep, replenish and govern the earth. They were given only one restriction – do not eat of the fruit of the tree in the middle of the garden. Following the theme of this book, this was a gate that they were meant to keep and they failed. Succumbing to the tempter – they ate of the fruit. It is very important to understand at this juncture that Adam and Eve could have reversed the curse that was about to fall on them. I believe that if the first Adam, like the second Adam (Jesus Christ) had stood up and intervened as a gatekeeper and asked for forgiveness the story would have been rewritten.

Instead, because of their sin and rebellion, Adam and Eve could no longer reside in the garden. They lost (or gave away) what had been given to them. And now cherubim guarded the gate. What were the cherubim guarding? What could Adam and Eve no longer experience?

## LIFE, INTIMACY AND REVELATION

We used to have a small plague hanging in our master bathroom which simply declared, "Of all the things I have lost – I miss my mind the most." Well Adam and Eve lost something greater. The cherubim of God were keeping Adam and Eve from at least three things. First, the cherubim guarded them from the fullness of **life**.

Man has eaten of the fruit. The curse of death has come upon them. The gate must be guarded so that they will not eat of the tree of life and experience an eternal life filled with curses. God desires the fullness of life and blessing for His children, but only He can bring us that life. The tree of life had to be guarded so that we could ultimately be redeemed into the fullness of life. God is the Creator and Giver of life and it can only come from Him. Life coming from any other source is counterfeit, hollow and meaningless. God will give us His life and the fullness of it, but He must do it in His time and on His terms for it to be valid. Anything less would indeed be less than what He intended for us.

Adam and Eve lost their fullness of life in God but they also lost **intimacy**. From the moment of the fall Adam and Eve no longer experienced intimacy and trust. Their relationship could no longer be described as "walking and talking" in the garden. Before the fall, they could hear Him in the quiet of the garden. They could respond to Him. But after they disobeyed Him, they no longer had that relationship. It had been replaced by fear, shame, rebellion and distrust. The true joy of salvation that you and I can experience is not just the knowledge that we have life in Jesus Christ but that we have a personal relationship with the Lord of the universe – a relationship defined by our ability to hear Him as He hears us.

The third thing (closely related to intimacy) that is no longer theirs is **the ability to receive revelation.** Because of their sin, there is no voice of God being heard. Therefore, there is no revelation. There is no vision. There is no prophecy. The King James Version rendering of Proverbs 29:18a declares: "Where there is no vision, the people perish." If you can't hear God, you don't know where you're going. If you can't perceive His heart than your life is empty and void of direction and purpose. Without revelation, we live (exist) from day to day and join the cry of the preacher from Ecclesiastes: "'Vanity of vanities,' says the Preacher; 'Vanity of vanities, all is vanity.' What profit has a man from all his labor in which he toils under the sun" (Ecclesiastes 1:2, 3)?

Everything was falling apart for Adam and Eve. They had lost life, intimacy and revelation. But God provided a covering. God provided a way. God desires His children to be at His side. God desires to speak into and through each of us. Whenever we find ourselves shut out, God establishes a gate, an opening or a door. He redeems that which is lost. He restores that which is torn down. He transforms chaos into order! He gives us a glimpse into heaven.

## THE GATE OF HEAVEN

The scene is Jacob running from his home in Beersheba. He has deceived his brother Esau out of his birthright and blessing. Tired and weary he places his head on a rock and falls asleep. He dreams of angels ascending and descending on a ladder into heaven. Read carefully Genesis 28:16-17: "Then Jacob awoke from his sleep and said, "Surely the LORD is in this place, and I did not know it." And he was afraid and said, "How awesome is this place! This is none other than the house of God, and this is the gate of heaven!"

The revelation of heaven and God that had been lost through Adam and Eve's rebellion was revealed to Jacob. Light pierced the darkness of Jacob's life. Hope and promise were released through the gate of heaven the Lord revealed to Jacob. Through this gate, the Lord was revealing His desire to restore **revelation** to Jacob and to us. God was revealing Himself to Jacob and in doing so was manifesting His desire to restore us to intimacy.

Look with me at Revelation 3:20: "Behold, I stand at the door and knock. If anyone hears My voice and opens the door, I will come in to him and dine with him, and he with Me." The Lord is inviting us to draw near. The Lord Himself is the gate (John 10) through whom we pass. He desires to eat and drink with us. He desires and restores **intimacy**. What a beautiful thought! The God of heaven and earth wants to be intimately acquainted with you and me. Through His Son He has restored us to that relationship which was lost in the garden.

Now read and meditate on this passage from the Book of Ruth.

Now Boaz went up to the gate and sat down there; and behold, the close relative of whom Boaz had spoken came by. So, Boaz said, "Come aside, friend, sit down here." So, he came aside and sat down. And he took ten men of the elders of the city, and said, "Sit down here." So, they sat down. Then he said to the close relative, "Naomi, who has come back from the country of Moab, sold the piece of land which belonged to our brother Elimelech. And I thought to inform you, saying, 'Buy it back in the presence of the inhabitants and the elders of my people. If you will redeem it, redeem it; but if you will not redeem it, then tell me, that I may know; for there is no one but you to redeem it, and I am next after you.'" And he said, "I will redeem it." Then Boaz said, "On the day you buy the field from the hand of Naomi, you must also buy it from Ruth the Moabitess, the wife of the dead, to perpetuate the name of the dead through his inheritance." And the close relative said, "I cannot redeem it for myself, lest I ruin my own inheritance. You redeem my right of redemption for yourself, for I cannot redeem it." Now this was the custom in former times in Israel concerning redeeming and exchanging, to confirm anything: one man took off his sandal and gave it to the other, and this was a confirmation in Israel. Therefore, the close relative said to Boaz, "Buy it for yourself." So, he took off his sandal. And Boaz said to the elders and all the people, "You are witnesses this day that I have bought all that was Elimelech's, and all that was Chilion's and Mahlon's, from the hand of Naomi. Moreover, Ruth the Moabitess, the widow of Mahlon, I have acquired as my wife, to perpetuate the name of the dead through his inheritance, that the name of the dead may not be cut off from among his brethren and from his position at the gate. You are witnesses this day. (Ruth 4:1-10).

Did you notice what took place at the gate? Boaz redeemed Ruth as his bride. The gate was the place of justice.

The gate was the place of redemption.

The gate was the place of alignment – a place for a person to be brought back into the destiny God intended.

It was a place where life was bought and brought back into order. Boaz received his inheritance so that the name of the dead would not be cut off from among his brethren. In faith, we are numbered among the brethren of Boaz. Redemption comes via the gates. Salvation is a legal transaction that someone has to pay or redeem. Jesus paid for our salvation at the gates. "Therefore, Jesus also, that He might sanctify the people with His own blood, suffered outside the gate. Therefore, let us go forth to Him, outside the camp, bearing His reproach" (Hebrews 13:12-13). Jesus restored **life.**

The Lord restored all that humankind lost through the gate of rebellion and sin—life, intimacy and revelation. But take note – in Christ Jesus we are now the gates. We are the lights representing the Lord (Matthew 5:14). We are the salt which He uses to flavor our world (Matthew 5:13). We are the aroma of life that the Lord desires the world to smell (2 Corinthians 2:16). We are the ambassadors (2 Corinthians 5:20). We are the priests (Exodus 19:6; Isaiah 61:6; Revelation 5:10). Listen to Dr. Cottle again: "This is why there is a Church, the body of Christ. We make God legal in the earth. How does it happen that God needs legal entry to that which He created? He gave the earth to Adam. Adam sold it in sin to the Devil."[38] In other words we have had our ability to govern the earth restored to us as well.

**God redeemed the earth with the blood of His Son.**
**He purchased the earth back from the enemy.**

## WHAT NOW DOES GOD REQUIRE OF US?

He requires us once again to do as He commanded in the beginning. We are to take dominion of that which is ours in Christ Jesus.

**The Lord is waiting for us (as gates) to invite Him in as the king of Glory so that the authority of His kingdom can be displayed on earth.**

God needs us. That is why we are here. He wants His kingdom and His will to come forth through us. It is the Spirit of the Lord living within us that acts as a gate allowing the revelation, intimacy and life of God to come into the world in which we live. He is waiting for us to open the doors to allow the aroma, life, sound and glory of heaven to be released in our homes, workplaces, churches, cities, regions and nations.

**The King of Glory will come, but He needs open gates and open doors.**

**The King of Glory will release His power, authority, light, salvation and revelation, but He needs gates.**

If you will allow it, the Lord will use you and impregnate you with dreams, visions, plans and purpose. Just as He used the gates (people) of the past, He will use you and me.

One closing thought. The Lord is not only the Gate; He is also the Gatekeeper. We are not only gates; we are also the keepers of the gates. So, get your keys and get ready to open the gates.

LET US PRAY

Father, in Christ Jesus You restored all that was lost. I offer thanks and praise for the wonders of Your love. But more importantly, You have filled me with the purpose and destiny You first gave to Adam and Eve. I pray that I will open up my heart to not only receive You as Lord but to release Your kingdom on this earth in response to restored life, intimacy and revelation. I am a gate. Use me to come into this place. Amen.

# 10

## Gatekeepers

*Blessed is the man who listens to me, watching daily at my gates,*
*waiting at the posts of my doors*

PROVERBS *8:34*

### KEEPERS OF THE KEYS

Over forty years ago, soon after my wife and I were married, my mother presented us with a needlework that she had stitched. It was a picture depicting the Coat of Arms for my family name – Schlueter. The name Schlueter or Schlüter in German is classified as an occupational name. The coat of arms depicts a shield with a lion at its center. In the lion's paw is a key. The name Schlueter literally means "gatekeeper, keeper of the keys or keeper of the keys to the prison." Years ago, I was thrilled with mom's gift. We have it hanging on the wall in our living room. But today, as the Lord has revealed His intentions to me – I am thoroughly excited about the needlework and about a destiny that God has given my family and me to be "gatekeepers" in His kingdom. Now the needlework is surrounded by an assorted number and style of keys and key rings that we have both found and received as gifts.

"Blessed is the man who listens to me,
Watching daily at my gates,
Waiting at the posts of my doors" (Proverbs 8:34).

## THE CHARACTERISTICS OF GATEKEEPERS

The gates and gatekeepers are at the heart of God's plan for this time in His kingdom. He blesses those who listen to Him. He blesses those who deliberately listen for His voice, His instructions, and His timing. He blesses those who watch daily at His gates. He blesses those who stand at faithful watch at the gates of the heart, home, workplace, church, government and nation. He blesses those who wait at His doorposts. He blesses those who watch at His gates.

**Gatekeepers are to be attentive and obedient!** The Hebrew word for "listen" in verse 34 is "shama" which means to hear intelligently. It has the implication of being attentive and obedient.[39] It can often be translated as to gather together, to consent, to consider, obeying, to give ear to, and to hear or perceive. The word is not referring to the natural process of receiving sounds into a physical ear. It implies an exercise in perceiving in one's heart what is being said and acting (or being obedient to) upon what was heard.

**Gatekeepers are to be on the lookout!** The Hebrew word for "watch" in this verse is "shaqad." It means "to be alert, i.e. sleepless; hence to be on the lookout (whether for good or ill)."[40] It is translated in the King James Version as watch, hasten, remain or wake. As gatekeepers, we are to be on the lookout. It brings to mind old war movies. Whether the setting was in World War II, the Old West or in medieval times, there was a person or persons assigned to keep the lookout. They were to watch for trouble. They were to keep their eyes open. They were stay awake. To fall asleep at their post was not only deadly for those over whom they watched, but oftentimes it meant a death sentence for the sentry or watchman. The Lord does not require us to stay awake for twenty-four hours a day, seven days a week. He does require that our ears and eyes (especially our spiritual ones) stay open – whether we are asleep or awake. Gatekeepers were to stay alert.

**Gatekeepers are to listen and watch!** In this same verse in Proverbs the word "shamar" is used to express "wait." The <u>Greek-Hebrew Key Word Study Bible</u> defines this word as follows: "to hedge around something (as with thorns), to keep, to guard (a garden, Genesis 2:15; 3:24; a flock, Genesis 30:31; a house, Ecclesiastes 12:3), to watch (as a watchman of cattle or sheep, 1 Samuel 17:20; as a prophet, Isaiah 21:11; 62:6), to keep safe, to preserve (1 Samuel 26:15,16; II Samuel 18:12; Job 2:6; Proverbs 6:22; 13:3), to protect (Genesis 28:15, 20; Psalm 12:7; 16:1; 25:20), to retain (Genesis 37:11; 41:35) to abstain oneself (Deuteronomy 4:9; Joshua 6:18), to observe (a covenant, Genesis 17:9,10; 18:19; the commandments of God, I Kings 11:10; the Sabbath, Isaiah 56:2,6; a promise, I Kings 3:6; 8:24,25), to regard, to attend, to be kept, to be guarded, to take heed, to beware, to revere (Psalm 31:6)."[41]

Interestingly "shamar" has the same connotations as "shaqad." The message is clear. Gatekeepers are to listen and watch. Let me put Proverbs 8:34 into my own words. Blessed are those who guard my gates with attentive ears and obedient hearts. Blessed are my gatekeepers as they constantly keep their spiritual ears and eyes open to what I am doing and where I am going. Blessed are the watchers at my door as they wait for Me and put a guarded hedge around all that I have entrusted to them to protect.

Gatekeepers have a tremendous responsibility. They have been given great authority. Not only are we the gatekeepers – we are the gates. Let me restate something from Chapter Nine. The King of Glory will release His power, authority, light, salvation and revelation, but He needs gates. The Lord will use you and impregnate you with dreams, visions, plans and purpose. Just as He used the gates (Nehemiah) of the past, He will use you and me.

## THE FUNCTIONS OF A GATEKEEPER

**Gatekeepers determine who can and cannot enter.** "Blessed are those who do His commandments, that they may have the right to the tree of life, and may enter through the gates into the city. But outside are dogs and sorcerers and sexually immoral and murderers and idolaters, and whoever loves and practices a lie" (Revelation 22:14-15).

My wife and I helped our youngest daughter, Amy, fill out her applications for college. She was a senior in high school, the valedictorian of her class and a teenager. That last word sometimes depicts the presence of such things as independence and procrastination. And we were facing those issues that night. It's important to get your applications done in a timely fashion in order to secure your admission, grants and scholarships. (That's obviously a "parent statement"). Our problem this particular evening was the application essays. There were three essays required for the application and two had been completed. Mom and daughter were both tired. Amy wanted to get the essay written but also wanted Mom to stay and type the essay as Amy spoke it out. I had "done my part" of the application and was leaving our home office. I actually wanted to clear out before the fireworks began. Amy was getting frustrated. My wife, Kay, was showing her fatigue. It was obviously time for Dad to leave. But as I was leaving, I felt compelled to do something. I lifted up my hand and declared peace over the room. I declared that God would intervene in their project. And then I exited with haste. I went on to more spiritual things – a football game on TV. About thirty minutes later Kay and Amy came out of the office smiling and laughing. How odd! I asked what was so funny. They announced that they had finished the essay. They had written it in record time. They had not argued. They considered it the best of the three required essays and they wanted me to read it over before they mailed it. I did. It was a marvelous and mistake-free essay.

**Gatekeepers have authority to let things in and to push things out.** In a brief moment authority was played out in a very simple and yet profound fashion. I believe the Lord had compelled me to act as a gatekeeper for my family. As I acted on His prompting, the presence of conflict, frustration and anger had to leave as God's peace, wisdom and strength entered. We have this authority as gatekeepers in our homes, workplaces, church and community. We need to be attentive to the Lord's promptings and be willing to act upon them.

**Gatekeepers act as judges and officers at the gates**. "You shall appoint judges and officers in all your gates, which the LORD your God gives you, according to your tribes, and they shall judge the people with just judgment. You shall not pervert justice; you shall not show partiality, nor take a bribe, for a bribe blinds the eyes of the wise and twists the words of the righteous. You shall follow what is altogether just, that you may live and inherit the land which the LORD your God is giving you" (Deuteronomy 16:18-20).

That night in my home there was a judgment made in my heart that an attitude that was contrary to God's desire was being manifested. God required me to act as a judge (gatekeeper) and to declare it out of order. I shared in the last chapter that we had visited the ancient city of Dan in northern Israel. When the king sat at the gate, he was obligated to judge what came in and what went out of his city. And he was bound to listen to God's heart regarding those judgments. Without getting into a long essay on the history of Israel, we need to simply remember that Dan was located in the Northern Kingdom of Israel after it had split from the Southern Kingdom of Judah. The northern regions refused to worship God in Jerusalem. They established their own places of worship. One of those was at Dan. The foundations of the altar where they had built a golden calf are still there. They made judgments that were not after God's heart. Their false judgments brought the Northern Kingdom of Israel to its demise. As a result of their rebellion, Israel was destroyed by Assyria.

**Gatekeepers stay at the gates**. "Also, the gatekeepers were at each gate; they did not have to leave their position, because their brethren the Levites prepared portions for them" (2 Chronicles 35:15b).

Gatekeepers are to watch the gates at all times. When I was young I was troubled by these kinds of statements. You are not to leave your position. You are to pray without ceasing. I grew up in a household filled with faith and love for God. I also grew up in the Lutheran Church. My father still serves as a Lutheran pastor at the age of eighty-six. His father served as a Lutheran pastor. I remember as a young child when I first heard about "praying without ceasing" how it troubled my spirit. You see, in my youthful mind I saw my dad or grandfather reading the long pastoral prayers from the altar. I imagined a group of elderly women gathered in a prayer circle reading from their prayer books. I could not comprehend why God would be so cruel as to ask me to do the same – unceasingly! When I was young, I thought as a child. I now realize and teach as a Spirit-filled Lutheran pastor that to pray unceasingly is to get our heart and spirit constantly tuned to God. Whether we are asleep or awake our spirit can be connected and filled with God's Holy Spirit. We can hear and sense His revelations whether they come during our wakening hours or as dreams during our sleep. We can and must realize that awake or asleep we are positioned by God as gatekeepers and that He will speak to a "listening heart" those things we need to perceive are trying to enter through our gates. I have shared with my congregation that unceasing prayer is keeping your spirit constantly poised toward God.

There is one more insight into this brief verse from 2 Chronicles. The gatekeepers did not have to leave their gates because their brethren provided portions for them. What a powerful demonstration of the body of Christ. Gate keeping is not a private matter whether it is in the city, church, home or your own heart. We are to be surrounded by brothers and sisters who are there to provide us help and support as we stay in place to provide the same for them.

**Gatekeepers guard and watch the gates.** "And I commanded the Levites that they should cleanse themselves, and that they should go and guard the gates, to sanctify the Sabbath day" (Nehemiah 13:22). "Blessed is the man who listens to me, watching daily at my gates, waiting at the posts of my doors" (Proverbs 8:34). As a gatekeeper, God has assigned you and me to guard and watch what no one else can guard or watch in the same capacity. As a husband and father, I am the only one in that position in my family. I must guard and watch my wife and children. My wife is the only mother in our household. I am the only senior Pastor of Prince of Peace Church. No one else can guard or watch in that capacity. If you are an employer or employee, no one else has your position. If you are a teacher or a student, no one else can guard from that same place where you stand or sit. In some settings, there are several persons watching or guarding the same thing together, but each person has a certain position or God-given perspective to their place of gate keeping. For example, I will watch over the congregation as its pastor, and so will the three elders that serve with me. They will watch and guard the same flock out of their own position, gifting and perspective. What gate or gates has God asked you to guard?

**Gatekeepers write on the gates.** "Hear, O Israel: The LORD our God, the LORD is one! You shall love the LORD your God with all your heart, with all your soul, and with all your strength. And these words which I command you today shall be in your heart. You shall teach them diligently to your children, and shall talk of them when you sit in your house, when you walk by the way, when you lie down, and when you rise up. You shall bind them as a sign on your hand, and they shall be as frontlets between your eyes. You shall write them on the doorposts of your house and on your gates" (Deuteronomy 6:4-9).

These verses define the standard by which we watch our gates. This was the standard or truth that the Northern Kingdom of Israel abandoned and which led to their fall. Everything centers in our Lord and God. Everything at the gates in our lives is to be judged by His written and revealed Word. Our gates are not to be judged by the reasoning of man. They are not to be left open to the popular opinion of humanity. Just last night we witnessed the results of national, state and local elections. The future of our nation was compared to how many states were red (Republican) and blue (Democrat). The direction of our congress was decreed as being set up by the number of seats held in the House of the Representatives and the Senate. These statements may be true if we see things only from a political point of view, but the nation's future will not be determined by red or blue, Republican or Democrat, but by the will of our heavenly Father as He is responded to or rebelled against by those who watch the gates of our government. And those who watch those gates include the President, the members of Congress, the Supreme Court, corporations and businesses of the nation, the body of Christ and every single citizen of the country. We are gates and gatekeepers that God desires to use in this hour to release His heart and will into our midst.

"...if My people who are called by My name will humble themselves, and pray and seek My face, and turn from their wicked ways, then I will hear from heaven, and will forgive their sin and heal their land" (2 Chronicles 7:14). This verse has been quoted as a standard for revival, transformation, restoration and judgments concerning our nation. The truth of this verse will be released when God's people, regardless of their position or status in life, will take seriously their roles as gatekeepers of the nation. We need to hear His voice and allow His light to pass through our gates in order to pierce the darkness of our nation, city, family, church and personal life.

**Gatekeepers keep the gates open.** "Therefore, your gates shall be open continually; they shall not be shut day or night, that men may bring to you the wealth of the Gentiles, and their kings in procession. For the nation and kingdom which will not serve you shall perish, and those nations shall be utterly ruined" (Isaiah 60:11, 12). A couple of years after we moved to Arlington, Texas our home was invaded in the middle of the night by a cat burglar. The title fits the purpose. His desire was not just to rob and steal but to do it with the greatest of courage and stealth. Many thieves will break into a home or business when no one is home or when property is left open and unprotected. This invasion was in the middle of the night. He entered our bedroom and master bath while we were asleep in bed. At some point, I woke up and scared him off, but not before he managed to take some valuable jewelry, my wallet and other assorted items. After the trauma of that night we became extremely conscience of locking doors and windows and making sure that everything was closed up.

As the Lord was revealing the purpose of gates and gatekeepers, I was confused with this command in Isaiah to keep the gates open at all times. If gates are meant to let things in and keep other things out – how can that happen if the gates are always open? When I first preached on this a couple of years ago I dealt with this text by simply saying "keep your gates open to God's revelation and don't let anything contrary to Him and His character enter in." But I never felt that that was the full truth on the matter. A few months ago, in one of my late-night moments with the Lord He downloaded something more. He revealed to my heart a couple of marvelous truths about this passage.

1. I am one of His gates and His gates are defined as praise and righteousness. As I draw near to Him in worship He allows me to

hear His heart. As a result, His praise and righteousness flows from His throne through me (the gate) into the darkness of the world. If the gates are closed, His praise, life and light cannot enter into the world through me. If I close my gates out of fear or in response to some past trauma I cannot and will not be used as an instrument of God's power. If I am more concerned about locking the doors to keep Satan out then opening the doors to release the power of God then I am failing as a gatekeeper. In other words – don't lock the gates in fear of Satan, but fling them open to release the power and light of God into your workplace, home, school, church, etc. And that very light will cause Satan to flee.

2. Verse twelve of Isaiah 60 declares that the doors are to remain open so that the "wealth of the gentiles" may be brought in. As we remain steadfast and immovable in the praise and righteous-ness of God, not only will the power of God be released into the world but the wealth and riches of the world meant for the king-dom of God will be brought into God's treasury. There have been many prophecies and words in the last few years concerning the transfer of wealth from the world into the kingdom of God. This promise will be manifested through believers who have positioned themselves as faithful gates and gatekeepers in God's kingdom. And this is not referring to our personal wealth but the wealth of the kingdom of God.

**Gatekeepers invite in the King of Glory.** "Lift up your heads, O you gates! And be lifted up, you everlasting doors! And the King of glory shall come in. Who is this King of glory? The LORD strong and mighty, the LORD mighty in battle. Lift up your heads, O you gates! Lift up, you everlasting doors! And the King of glory shall come in. Who is this King of glory? The LORD of hosts, He is the King of glory" (Psalm 24:7-10).

In the summer of 2007, my wife Kay and I, at the mandate of the Lord, drove the circumference of the state of Texas. The primary purpose of the assignment was to invite the King of Glory into the state.

Inviting the King of Glory to come in is our greatest assignment and privilege as gatekeepers. If you do anything as a watcher of the gates – do this! And do it over and over. This is not meant to be a one-time request.

"King of Glory – come in!"

"Lord, come into my heart."

"Jesus, come into my home."

"King of kings, come into my workplace!"

"Lord of lords, come into my school!"

"My strong and mighty Lord, come into my church!"

"Lord, mighty in battle, come into our city!"

You can have a great ministry with just this one assignment. As you are driving home from work, invite the King of Glory to enter every physical gate you pass through. As you travel throughout your city, your home, down your street, or through the shopping mall, invite the King of Glory to come in. Who is this King of Glory? He is the Lord of hosts. He is Yahweh-Sabaoth. He is the Lord of all the hosts of heaven and we are inviting Him and the angelic forces of heaven to come through our gates. Our city or home or nation will be impacted by His arrival. Amen. Invite Him in! Stop right now in your reading and invite the King of Glory to enter your gates.

**Gatekeepers usher the city into its promised rest.** "Therefore, he said to Judah, 'Let us build these cities and make walls around them, and towers, gates, and bars, while the land is yet before us, because we have sought the LORD our God; we have sought Him, and He has given us rest on every side.' So, they built and prospered" (2 Chronicles 14:7).

As we seek His face and build up the gates and walls, God will bring forth rest into our lives. This rest does not imply a lack of activity, but an alignment with God's purposes. When we live and have our being in God, our lives come into a destiny, a purpose and a position designed by God. When we seek His face; our city, our nation begins to transform into God's design for that city or nation. God has a destiny for us.

"For I know the thoughts that I think toward you, says the LORD, thoughts of peace and not of evil, to give you a future and a hope" (Jeremiah 29:11).

"In Him also we have obtained an inheritance, being predestined according to the purpose of Him who works all things according to the counsel of His will, that we who first trusted in Christ should be to the praise of His glory" (Ephesians 1:11-12).

These verses speak of a future, a plan, a destiny, a hope, a pattern and a purpose that God has laid out for each of us as individuals and together as the body of Christ. As we allow our gates to be built up and established in Him, we come further and further into that promised future and destiny. Watch your gates! Keep your gates open! Invite the King of glory to come in! Stay continually at your gates and write upon them the Word and promises of God.

## LET US PRAY!

Lord, I open the gates. Come in with all Your might and power. Go forth through these gates with kingdom authority, grace, mercy and salvation. I will write Your promises on the gates. I watch them constantly. I will direct or poise my spirit towards You. Bring us to our promised rest and alignment as Your bride. Amen.

# 11

## Acting as a Gate

*"I will place you in places where you will release who I am into the world."*

(PERSONAL JOURNAL OF PASTOR TOM SCHLUETER)[42]

### YOU ARE A GATE!

Inviting the King of Glory to come in is our greatest assignment and privilege as gate- keepers. The understanding of gate assign- ments became very real to me on a trip I took to Papua New Guinea and China in January of 2005.

The Lord had already told me before the trip that He was going to put me into "appointed positions" to pray for certain persons and situations. I kept my eyes and ears open to Him. It is clear now that He indeed made divine appointments for me.

In Lae, Papua New Guinea, I was utterly amazed at what the Lord had accomplished through our friend Bapa Bomoteng. When we first met at Christ for the Nations in Dallas, Texas, Bapa had shown tremendous faith and perseverance by coming to Texas amid several personal and profes- sional trials. Our congregation, touched by Bapa's humble spirit and bold faith in Jesus, supported him through school, ordained him and sent him back to Papua New Guinea to serve the Lord. Now, just a few years later

Bapa is leading the largest church in Lae and is connected with almost every major missionary organization in the region. It was pure joy to pray over him and to speak blessings to all of his connections. I thought the Lord was beginning to define His word about "appointed positions" to me.

In China, the most significant moment came when we were taking a tour of the Forbidden City in Beijing. I had never been in China and enjoyed this first-time tour of the country. As we entered the Forbidden City through its massive ornate gates, the Lord spoke to my heart and said: "I will place you in places where you will release who I am into the world." He impressed upon me to study the gates. He commanded me to watch and to be alert. I did, but I received no further revelation that day. The next morning as I awakened the Lord clearly spoke to me again, "Watch very carefully today."

I knew we were going to tour the Great Wall and the Ming tombs. In my thoughts, I started comparing the Great Wall to the walls of Nehemiah. I just knew what the Lord was thinking and what He was going to show me. Word of advice – do not tell the Lord you know what He is thinking. He will come back with something like "My thoughts are higher than your thoughts."

We were not yet at the Great Wall, but were down in the tomb of the thirteenth and last emperor in the Ming dynasty when the Lord started stirring my spirit. He pointed out to me the dominant presence of dragons and the strong emphasis on the number "six." To the Chinese, the dragon represents the emperor – the king of the land. In the Bible, the dragon characterizes the beast – Satan. The number six in the Hebrew language represents man, but it can also represent Satan because it falls short of the complete number "seven." As we walked through the tomb, the Lord opened my eyes to see that there were six dragons encased in the side of the emperor's crown and dragons were sculpted on the back of each of the three thrones set up in a row – one for the emperor, one for his wife and one for his concubine. The dragons' heads extended up and over the back of the thrones.

At one point, the Lord began to remind me of all the gates we had passed through at the tombs as well as at the Forbidden City. I found all of this fascinating, but sensed the Lord had not yet given me the complete revelation. I kept on listening and watching.

Enlightenment came near the end of the tour of the tombs in the museum. We felt compelled to go into the museum. We might have felt compelled because we were freezing. The temperature was below zero and any warm room was cherished. The walls of the museum were covered with pictures of national leaders from all around the world who had been in the tombs. We immediately identified President Nixon and President Carter, who had visited while they were in office. There were pictures of leaders from Austria, the Netherlands, Australia, England, Germany and the United States – around 50 of them. They had all visited the tombs, and in the photographs, they were all touching and smiling at statues of the dragon which signified the rule of the emperor.

Suddenly the Lord commanded, "Break the ties." At that moment, I felt like the least qualified person in the world to do so, but I stepped out in faith and obediently began to pray. In a covert fashion, I walked by each picture and quietly decreed that any assignment that had been made against these nations be broken in the name of Jesus. No one knew what I was doing, but I sensed a very real release in my spirit that something had taken place. All of a sudden, I had a wonderful revelation. I was a gate. God was using me. It was not about me. It was about the Lord. He was just looking for someone to act as a door or a gateway through which He, the King of Glory, could enter.

This revelation was confirmed the next year when I heard Dutch Sheets speak at a city-wide prayer gathering at Gateway Church in Southlake, Texas. Dutch told how in the year 2000 the Lord had commanded him to go the Northeast region of the United States and "turn it" in the Spirit. He was to act as a gatekeeper and open up this door for God to move into the region. Dutch shared that this had been a brand-new experience for him, and he had told the Lord he would "give it his best shot." The Lord answered him back that he was not looking for Dutch's best shot. He was looking for his obedience.[43]

When we think we are not qualified to be a gate or when we tell the Lord we will try our best, the focus is all on us. Acting as a gate is not about us. It is all about Him.

The King of Glory will come into your home, your city, or your nation,
but He needs gates.
God will release His power, authority, light, salvation and revelation,
but He needs gates.
The Lord will impregnate you with dreams, visions, plans and purposes,
but He needs gates to allow those dreams and purposes to spring forth.

The experience as a tourist I described in China was simply a gate assignment. At a certain time and place God needed a gate. He needed someone to invite the true King to come in. I don't know what has happened because of that obedient act, but of one thing I am certain – the King of Glory came into that place, and connections between the dragon and those nations were broken by His power. In September of 2007 while attending a Tuesday morning prayer at Glory of Zion International Ministries in Denton the Lord spoke through me and I declared, "The gates of China will open. On 8-8-08 at 8 PM the gates will open in Beijing." At 8 o'clock PM on August 8, 2008 (during the year of the gates) the gates will open in Beijing as they host the Summer Olympics. The kingdom of God will enter through those gates that have been opened by prayer and declaration.

The effect of our assignments on the darkness of the world was clearly demonstrated as we headed down a two-lane road bordered by a deep ditch filled with beautiful hardwood trees. The ground was icy and frozen. The scenery reminded me of scenes in the movie Dr. Zhivago. All of a sudden, we saw a large truck coming from the opposite direction and behind it a car trying to pass. It was one of those moments when you know there is not enough space. The car was coming at us at the same speed in which we were traveling. It was happening so fast that all options were gone. The oncoming car could not pull back. The truck could not move over. We were going to hit the truck, the car or the hardwood trees in the ice-covered ditch. At the last second, our driver veered towards the ditch. I was seated in the front passenger seat, and all I remember was crying out to Jesus as I saw the ditch beneath me. Instantaneously, our car was back on the road on the other side of the oncoming car and truck. The Lord had literally picked us up and moved us. There was no other explanation.

Oddly, I remember looking at my watch. I was not surprised on returning home to discover that several friends, family members and intercessors had been awakened at that same hour in the middle of night to pray.

That night in my bed in the hotel room I looked up and saw a movement of light in the room. None of the curtains were open and no night lights were on. I kept peering into the area above my bed. I watched the room fill up with a moving cloud -- just floating in our room. I was wide awake and reaching up into it. The cloud was there only a moment, but it left me with an overwhelming sense of peace. I went to sleep assured that God had been watching over us and that our team had fulfilled our "gate assignment."

Gate assignments are not new in God's kingdom. I believe Jesus gave us an understanding of gates when He was journeying with His disciples in the region of Caesarea Philippi.

"And I also say to you that you are Peter, and on this rock, I will build My church, and the gates of Hades shall not prevail against it. And I will give you the keys of the kingdom of heaven, and whatever you bind on earth will be bound in heaven, and whatever you loose on earth will be loosed in heaven" (Matthew 16:18-19).

The Lord is building His church. He is releasing His kingdom on earth. He declares that He will build His church and the gates of Hades (Hell) will not prevail against it. When I consider that verse, all of these images of Ming's tomb, the Forbidden City and that road in China come to my mind. The gates of Hell are just like the gates of Heaven, but what comes through the gates of Hell are the powers, manifestations, principalities and forces of evil. Those gates, Jesus said, will not prevail against the gates of God. They will not prevail! Declare it – they will not prevail. Regardless of what is thrown at us, it will not prevail. Our lives might be threatened or even taken, but the gates of Hell will not prevail against the kingdom of God.

But hold on a moment! Let's not get this backwards. I do not believe for one moment that our posture as the Church is defensive. Let me remind you of what I wrote in the last chapter. "As I draw near to Him in worship He allows me to hear His heart. As a result, His praise and righteousness flows from His throne through me (the gate) into the darkness of the world. If the gates are closed, His praise, life and light cannot enter into the world through me. If I close my gates out of fear or in response to some past trauma I cannot and will not be used as an instrument of God's power. If I am more concerned about locking the doors to keep Satan out then opening the doors to release the power of God then I am failing as a gatekeeper. In other words – don't lock the gates in fear of Satan, but fling them open to release the power and light of God into your workplace, home, school, church, etc."

Bill Johnson in his book <u>The Supernatural Power of a Transformed Mind</u> in commenting on Matthew 16:18-19 writes:

When I was younger, I read this wrong somehow and thought it meant that "the gates of heaven will prevail against the assault of the enemy." That fit my theology better back then. I saw the Church as a group of people locked inside a compound, shoulders against the gate, trying to hold the fort as the devil and his powerful minions beat against it. I saw the Church in a posture of fear and weakness, trying to protect what we had until God hurried up and rescued us from the big, bad devil. But Jesus gave us an opposite picture. He said, "The gates of hell will not prevail." Has it ever occurred to you that we're on offense, not defense? The principalities and powers that set up dominions or "gates" all over the earth will not prevail against us! We are advancing and winning, and Jesus promises that in the end, no gate of hell will stand. Wow![44]

Take time right now to apply this truth personally. What gates of hell have been opening up in your life? Are there gates of illness, financial destruction, fear? Declare out loud that those gates will not prevail against the advances of the kingdom of God!

Are forces of evil coming through the gates of hell against you, your family, your neighborhood, your workplace? Declare now that the kingdom of Light will prevail against the kingdom of darkness. His light, healing, provision, strength and life will prevail against and destroy the works of the enemy.

## DECREE THE LORD'S PROMISE

We are gates and gatekeepers of God's kingdom. God desires to release His kingdom into and through us – personally and corporately – individually and as a church. We cannot miss this point! We are gates. We have been qualified by Jesus to be portals for God's kingdom to be manifested on earth. Bill Johnson writes:

The only way to consistently do Kingdom works is to view reality from God's perspective. That's what the Bible means when it talks about renewing our minds. The battle is in the mind. The mind is the essential tool in bringing Kingdom reality to the problems and crisis people face. God has made it (the mind) to be the gatekeeper of the supernatural. To be of any use to the Kingdom, our mind must be transformed. (Emphasis mine) [45]

Renew your mind. Don't question your abilities. Set your eyes and ears on the Lord. Wait on the move, the impulse, the word, the timing and the direction of the Lord and be a gate!

"You will make your prayer to Him,
He will hear you,
And you will pay your vows.
You will also declare a thing,
And it will be established for you;
So, light will shine on your ways" (Job 22:27-28).

This is a very powerful and popular verse today, but we must take care in understanding it. This verse translated literally instructs us in Hebrew to "decree a promise or word."[46] We are to decree what has already been spoken or promised through the written or rhema word of God. These decrees are not based on something we desire, but on what God desires and what He has spoken or promised. That is worth repeating: These decrees are not based on what we desire, but on what God desires. In other words, God has decreed or declared something that will bring forth His kingdom and His will on earth. He reveals to His saints what He has decreed, and we, in turn, decree it and release it into our world. We act as gates through which His Word and His light can pass. When we act as gates, His word and His decreed promise will be released and brought to fullness in our homes, workplaces, cities and nations. Let us close out this chapter with prayer, but let our prayers be the decrees of what the Lord has promised to us. I invite you to pray along as you read the following prayer but let it be a catapult into your own season of decrees and declarations.

## PRAYER OF DECLARATION

Father, we lift up Your name. You are mighty to deliver and to save. Lord, thank You for calling us Your gates. We take our place as your ambassadors, priests, servants and kings, allowing You to move through us. We want all the focus off of us and on You. We want no credit. We desire for You to receive all the glory. Open our ears to hear You. Open our eyes to see You. Open up our hearts to perceive Your ways.

Lord, at Your command and desire, we open up our gates and invite the King of Glory to come in. And at Your word we also decree Your promises. Our decrees which are based on Your promises will prevail against and destroy the works of the enemy.

We decree Your kingdom come and Your will be done.

We decree that the power and kingdom of God will penetrate and dispel the darkness that surrounds us.

We decree the transformation of our lives and the lives of our family.

We decree the restoration and rebuilding of our homes, businesses, cities and nation.

We decree the release of healing and deliverance into the lives of people.

We decree the salvation of God to be released over the region in which we live! Lord, wherever You come, let Your light, salvation and revelation be released into that place. Let Your kingdom come and Your will be done in Jesus' name. Amen.

# 12

# The Opposition – Part One

*And I also say to you that you are Peter, and on this rock, I will build My church,*
*and the gates of Hades shall not prevail against it. And I will give you the keys of the kingdom of heaven, and whatever you bind on earth will be bound in heaven,*
*and whatever you loose on earth will be loosed in heaven*

MATTHEW *16:18-19*

## GOD'S PERFECT PLAN FOR GATES

The walls of our families, churches, cities, states and nations are being rebuilt, transformed, renewed, and restored. And in Jesus we are the gates. We are the intermediaries, the priests. We stand in the gap. The King of Glory will come in, but He must have gates through which to enter. God will release His power, authority, light, salvation and revelation, but He needs gates. Just as the Lord used the gates (people) of the past, He will use you and me.

But the enemy also has gates. Listen to the Lord in Matthew 16:17-19:

"And Jesus answered and said to him, 'Blessed are you, Simon Barjona, because flesh and blood did not reveal this to you, but My Father who is in heaven. And I also say to you that you are Peter, and upon this rock I will build My church; and the gates of Hades shall not overpower it. I will give you the keys of the kingdom of heaven; and whatever you shall bind on earth shall be bound in heaven, and whatever you shall loose on earth shall be loosed in heaven'" (Matthew 16:17-19).

Our prayer group was standing at the foot of the cliffs at Caesarea Philippi in northern Israel. It is the site of one of three headwaters that flow into the Jordan River. It is the site of Peter's confession. In the cliffs, there is a huge cave and ruins of an ancient cultic temple that honored the god Pan. We were finishing our time at the site and I was teaching on gates and God's desire that we would take authority against the powers of evil and the gates of hell. At that moment our tour guide, Yossi, stepped up to me and declared, "Yes, and that's the gate of hell." I asked for clarification. He pointed at the cave and shared that traditionally (I recognize that this is an often-used word on Israel tours) this cave was called the gate of hell. It is believed by some as the site that marks the throwing down of Satan and his minions to earth. The cultic temple on the site venerated Pan. Pan is the Greek god of shepherds and flocks, of mountain wilds, hunting and rustic music. He has the hindquarters, legs, and horns of a goat. Pan inspired disorder and fear which resulted in the word 'panic' being attributed to him. The word pandemonium also comes from him. He represents confusion, panic and fear. Of course, Pan was later known for his music, capable of arousing inspiration, sexuality, or panic, depending on his intentions.[47]

Caesarea Philippi is in the foothills of Mount Hermon which is also believed by some as the site of our Lord's transfiguration. Regardless of where things "really took place" there was a sudden leaping in my heart that acknowledged that the Lord was reminding us and imparting to us the power of the keys.

## THE OFFICE OF THE KEYS

This principle regarding the power of the keys is at the heart of God's plan for gatekeepers. In Matthew 16:17-19 Jesus is restoring us to our destiny lost in the garden. He is giving us His authority to bind and loose. He is giving us the authority to enforce that which He carried out on the cross.

In my Lutheran heritage, this is called "The Office of the Keys." It refers to the authority that each Christian has been given to forgive or not to forgive – to bind or to loose. But even though it includes forgiveness it goes much deeper and further.

In his book, Prayer is Invading the Impossible, Jack Hayford gives the following as a definition of supplication: "Supplication reaches to call forth from the Almighty the reinstatement of His original decree in whatever matters we bring before Him."[48] Supplication (and in our case – the office of the keys) is crying out to God—asking Him to keep His will regarding issues that have been already settled in His heart. And everything regarding supplication centers on the cross of Jesus Christ.

Hayford goes on to say: "There is nothing for which I shall supplicate—nothing for which I shall plead the establishing of God's eternally intended order—but that the right to ask is granted and the power to answer is released through His cross."[49]

The Lord is building a people—an army if you will–that will be conformed and shaped into His image. Their purpose will be assault the "gates of hell" and the gates of hell (the plots, strategies, assignments and plundering of the evil realm) will not prevail against the Church. And He gives us the keys (the authority to open or lock) those gates of Hell. Whatever we bind on earth will be bound in heaven, and whatever we loose on earth will be loosed in heaven. In other words—as His representatives (gatekeepers) and His authority (keys) we are to bind up or loose that which is on His heart.

We accept the fact that God has declared and decreed that certain matters are settled. Whenever we are faced with situations or circumstances where His heart, His mercy, His righteousness, His holiness, and His character and purposes are obviously not ruling, we pray—we supplicate. Our prayer is a declaring, decreeing, calling forth of what He has **willed** and (here is an extremely important aspect) **cannot be released** on earth until someone calls for it.

Jesus tells us that whatever we bind on earth will be bound in heaven. Let us look a bit at these Greek words. The Greek verb "to bind" is "deo."[50] It is aorist in tense, subjunctive in mood and active in voice. What does all that mean? At a given point in time (aorist tense) you might or might not (subjunctive mood) carry out a conscious, responsible act (voice). In other words—whatever you decide to bind at a given point in time will be bound. The phrase "will be bound" is "dedemenon." Shall be bound is the future, passive participle of "deo."[51] In other words it speaks of a completed act (future) performed by another (passive). Listen to how Jack Hayford amplifies these words of Jesus: "Whatever you may at any time encounter (of hell's counsels which the Church shall prevail against), you will then face a decision as to whether you will or won't bind it. What transpires will be conditional upon your response. If you do personally and consciously involve yourself in the act of binding the issue on earth, you will discover that at that future moment when you do, that it has already been bound in heaven!"[52]

## THE GATES OF HELL

The gates of hell will come against us but the Lord has given us, as gates, the ability in His name to prevail against hell and all its minions. The word "Hades" in Greek is translated as Hades, hell or grave but the literal translation is "unseen" or "hidden." The root word "eido" is the word "to see or to know."[53] God is giving us the authority to release His light, life and revelation into the darkness, the fear, the panic and the pandemonium of the world.

As we declared in the last chapter, the gates of Hades (Hell) cannot prevail against us. In the strength of the Lord we will overcome the devouring tactics of the enemy. Even so, the enemy will use devouring tactics. The gates of hell have the same function as the gates of Heaven. Gates are portals for something to pass through and when someone allows themselves to be used as a gate of Hell, the evils of darkness are manifested. And those evils will be manifested against the kingdom of God. BUT EVIL CAN NOT OVERPOWER OR PREVAIL AGAINST US!

As we turn to the fourth through sixth chapters of Nehemiah we discover that Nehemiah is leading the people in the reconstruction of the walls of Jerusalem, and he once again comes face to face with his enemies – Sanballat, Tobiah and Geshem the Arab. We introduced these names in Chapter Seven but now their tactics are becoming fierce. As you read this chapter keep in mind that the enemy will fight with persistence. Also, be mindful that a heart turned to God in prayer will succeed in victory over every plot devised by the enemy. And finally, you will be reminded that ultimately, we do not fight against flesh and blood but against the principalities of darkness (hell).

## THE ENEMY WILL TRY TO STOP US

In the book of Nehemiah, the opposition to God's plan is represented by Sanballat -- the satrap or governor of Samaria, Tobiah – his "yes" man and Geshem the Arab -- a powerful tribal chieftain from the Persian province of Arabia. This evil trio watches everything that Nehemiah does and accuses him of rebellion against King Artaxerxes and the gods of Persia. The text defines the mood of Sanballat.

Sanballat was furious, burning up with jealousy. He was angry to the point of rage. His mocking communication with Nehemiah was accompanied by a scornful intimidating laugh. Be aware that the enemy will use a variation of this scheme against us – the gates of the Lord – that he employed to prevent the building up of the gates in the book of Nehemiah.

## THE ENEMY WILL TRY TO DEMORALIZE THE BUILDERS.

To set the stage for Sanballat's tactics I need to take you back to Numbers 22-25. There we find the story of Balaam. Balaam, a sorcerer, is hired by Balak of the Moabites to come and curse Israel as they journey out of the wilderness into the Promised Land. I will share a brief summary of what is going on, but please take the time to meditate on this story. This is the first time that Israel is faced with the evil principality Baal. Let me share some basic facts regarding Baal that Dutch Sheets mentions in a Prayer Newsletter that he published on March 2, 2007. He writes:

Through a season of tremendous warfare in November and December, as well as confirmation from many key leaders, God has exposed the spirit of Baal as one of the strongmen—perhaps the strongman—over America.

- Baal-hamon, one of Baal's names, means "the lord of wealth or abundance." Chuck Pierce believes, and I agree, that this is the principality warring against the great transfer of wealth to the church. You must war against this spirit to see your inheritance released.

- Baal-berith, another of his names, means "the lord of the covenant." The Hebrew word baal actually means "husband" or "marriage." This spirit always attempted to cause Israel to "divorce" or break covenant with God and "marry" or align with him. Consistent with this, in so many ways America has broken covenant with God and married Baal. This is, I believe, the strongman behind most covenant-breaking.

- Baal is the strongman behind sexual perversion. Homosexuality was and is one of his big strongholds. I believe all of the sexual sin and perversion in America is, to one degree or another, under Baal's orchestration. You will continue to see God expose leaders in the church who aligned themselves with this spirit. Pray for the church to be cleansed and for Baal's hold on America in this area to be broken.

- Baal always goes after the next generation, trying to cut off the extension of God's covenantal purposes. He is a violent spirit and even required human sacrifice. Abortion is under Baal, as is the "cutting" of today's young generation (see 1 Kings 18:28), the vampire and goth movement, and the death culture in general that has so invaded America. Baal is leading the fight to avert the great awakening planned for the young generation of Americans today. Pray against and bind these efforts.

- Witchcraft and occult spirits in general operate under Baal. So, does Jezebel.[54]

Baal attempted through Balak and Balaam to curse Israel. Baal attempted to cut off Israel's inheritance. He attempted to marry himself to the nation in order to destroy it and its destiny. The curses of Balaam were turned into blessings. Israel prospered as Baal was defeated. But in Numbers 25, Baal again attempted to devour Israel. This time it was a direct attack as harlots were introduced into the ranks of Israel. Baal was unleashed and a plague traveled through the tribes of God's people. It was not stopped until Phinehas, the priest, literally drove a spear through a man and his harlot. Israel waged a continual war against this foe. Study the lives of Gideon and Elijah. To make a very long and sad story short, it seemed that Baal eventually won as the people of Israel end up exiled in Babylon (the very heart of Islam is a Baal structure). And now we see that they returned and Israel had to once again face this formidable foe. Baal once again sought to cut off their destiny. Baal seeks to curse rather than bless. He seeks to introduce panic, confusion and pandemonium. And this time Baal uses Sanballat, Tobiah and Geshem. Listen to their beguiling words.

- What are these feeble Jews doing?" Sanballat asked. The Hebrew word for "feeble" is "'amelal" and refers to someone who is sick, weak and languid.[55] Sanballat was telling his troops in earshot of the Jews that they were helpless.
- Will they fortify themselves? Some translations read "will they restore for themselves?" The Amplified Bible reads: "Will they restore things at will and by themselves"? In other words, the enemy will try to get the focus on self. There is a mocking tone to this question. Are you so self-centered and prideful as to think you can you can do this? It's all about you. You are doing this, not for your God but for yourselves. Can you possibly do this on your own? You are weak and feeble.
- Will they offer sacrifices? The enemy will belittle our faith and devotion to God. The sacrificial system was the bonding element of the Jewish faith community. This taunt was meant to be a direct "slam" against the faith of the Jews
- Can they finish in a day? The enemy will introduce hopelessness based on the length of time it will take to accomplish this enormous task. He questions the strength of their commitment. The enemy has already called them weak and feeble. Now he adds hopelessness. Do you have any idea how long this is going to take? Do you expect the status of this city to turn around overnight?

- Can they revive the stones from the dusty rubble even the burned ones?" The Hebrew word for revive is chayah. It means to live or to revive. It is also translated: to keep or make alive, to give the promise of life, to nourish or preserve, to quicken, restore and repair or to make whole.[56] Did they really believe they could make their city – the city of Jerusalem – come back to life? Can God restore, repair and revive a city through His people? Can you take burned up rubbish and create new life?
- Even what they are building — if a fox should jump on it, he would break their stone wall down! Tobiah joins in the mocking. The enemy will point out the futility of our work and our purpose. Go ahead and do your work. It will be just as feeble as you are!

Does this all sound familiar? The enemy will be relentless. He will mock and defy you as he has mocked and defied Israel in the wilderness. He will mock and defy you as he has mocked and defied our God.

"And those who passed by blasphemed Him, wagging their heads and saying, 'You who destroy the temple and build it in three days, save Yourself! If You are the Son of God, come down from the cross.' Likewise, the chief priests also, mocking with the scribes and elders, said, 'He saved others; Himself He cannot save. If He is the King of Israel, let Him now come down from the cross, and we will believe Him. He trusted in God; let Him deliver Him now if He will have Him; for He said, 'I am the Son of God.' Even the robbers who were crucified with Him reviled Him with the same thing" (Matthew 27:39-44).

## NEHEMIAH'S RESPONSE – PRAYER

Hear, O our God, how we are despised! Return their reproach on their own heads and give them up for plunder in a land of captivity. Do not forgive their iniquity and let not their sin be blotted out before Thee, for they have demoralized the builders. So, we built the wall and the whole wall was joined together to half its height, for the people had a mind to work. (Nehemiah 4:4-6)

Nehemiah's response to all this harassment was to pray. He never left his first call. It was prayer that brought him to this point and it was his intimate communion and communication with God that carried him through to victory. We oftentimes forsake this central strategy. We know that God brought us into this place, but at some point, we start to believe that we must now fight with our own strength. We begin to take on Satan and his forces with our own strategies or with strategies we have learned from our study or from watching others. Instead, we must pray in order to receive God's fresh strategies as well as understanding Satan's tactics. While it behooves us to know our enemy and to know his best-known strategies, we must not fall into the trap of assuming he won't pull a new one on us. Nehemiah as well as other warriors of the Old Testament – especially Joshua and David – reveals to us the necessity of seeking God's new strategy for each battle. Although similar tactics may be anticipated, no two battles were alike. We have to go back to the Commander for the battle plan because He is the only one who sees the whole battlefield.

Nehemiah pleaded with God to take care of the enemy. Notice that Nehemiah did not argue with those who opposed him. He did not curse them. He confidently called on God to move against His enemies. Vengeance belongs to God.

- Psalm 54:4-5—**God will repay**: "Behold, God is my helper; the Lord is with those who uphold my life. He will repay my enemies for their evil. cut them off in Your truth.
- Psalm 94:1-3—**God will judge**: "LORD God, to whom vengeance belongs—O God, to whom vengeance belongs, shine forth! Rise up, O Judge of the earth; render punishment to the proud. LORD, how long will the wicked triumph?

The battle is all about God's vengeance – not ours. Everything within us is driven by God's love, but God's love does not tolerate injustice and evil. We war not against flesh and blood but against all forces of evil. Moses' true enemy was not Pharaoh. Nehemiah's true enemy was not Sanballat and Tobiah. Jesus' true enemy was not the Pharisees.

"Beloved, do not <u>avenge yourselves</u>, but rather <u>give place to wrath</u>; for it is written, "Vengeance is Mine, I will repay," says the Lord. Therefore "If your enemy is hungry, feed him; if he is thirsty, give him a drink; for in so doing you will heap coals of fire on his head" (Romans 12:19-20).

## CLOSING THOUGHTS

God has made us gatekeepers. We hold the keys to the downfall of these enemies. In the next chapter, we will continue with the strategies of Sanballat, Tobiah and Geshem, but in closing out this chapter let it be stated that...

**God has appointed us to proclaim His righteous judgments.** God will use us to prevail against the enemies of His kingdom. We will move by the power of His Spirit.

"The Spirit of the Lord GOD is upon Me, because the LORD has anointed Me to preach good tidings to the poor; He has sent Me to heal the brokenhearted, to proclaim liberty to the captives, and the opening of the prison to those who are bound; to proclaim the acceptable year of the LORD, and the day of vengeance of our God" (Isaiah 61:1-2)

**It is God, not man, whom we fear.** Nehemiah did not fear his opponents. He feared God. It was that fear which drove him to his knees in prayer. It was that fear that caused him to persevere against the enemy.

"For we know Him who said, "Vengeance is Mine, I will repay," says the Lord. And again, "The LORD will judge His people." It is a fearful thing to fall into the hands of the living God" (Hebrews 10:29-31).

## NEHEMIAH'S RESPONSE -- CONTINUE TO BUILD.

It was that fear of God which encouraged the people to continue the building. They had a mind to build. We so often get into our own battle with the enemy and at that moment—he has won—for the work that the Lord set before us is stalled and incomplete. Call God to the battle. Set your mind to build by His Spirit. And know that the battle never ceases.

LET US PRAY

Father, You have called us to the frontlines of Your kingdom. Just as the Israelites were poised to enter into their promised land so we are poised to enter into our promises. The enemy will seek to confuse us. He will seek to devour our destiny with curses, fear, panic and distraction. We set our eyes on You. Give us the strategies and tactics needed to perceive and destroy the enemy that comes against us. We will prevail against the enemy. We are the gates of Your kingdom. Fill us anew with Your Spirit. Give us a mind to pray. Give us a mind to build. In Jesus' name. Amen.

# 13

# The Opposition – Part Two

*On that day, they read from the Book of Moses in the hearing of the people, and in it was found written that no Ammonite or Moabite should ever come into the assembly of God, because they had not met the children of Israel with bread and water, but hired Balaam against them to curse them. However, our God turned the curse into a blessing. So, it was, when they had heard the Law, that they separated all the mixed multitude from Israel.*

*(NEHEMIAH 13:1-3)*

## THE ONGOING PLOTS OF THE ENEMY

On April 21, 2007 members of the Trinity Apostolic Prayer Network as well as apostolic, pastoral and intercessory leaders from Oklahoma, Kansas and around the state of Texas gathered in Olney, Texas. Olney is a small and seemingly insignificant town about two hours west of Fort Worth. But from a piece of property in Olney three major rivers in Texas are fed – the Trinity, the Brazos and the Red. The Trinity Apostolic Prayer Network is a gathering and connecting of apostolic leaders to bring forth transformation, unity and healing to the Dallas/Fort Worth region and the entire Trinity River watershed. The network will depend on God directing them prophetically as they approach Him in worship and prayer. The members desire to see the redemptive anointing of the region to flow freely. They desire the people, the history, the culture, and the destiny of the Trinity River basin to be transformed as the Lord is enthroned in their midst.

Leaders gathered in Olney to decree a divorce[57] from the principality of Baal. It sounds Old Testament in nature, but we are standing firm against the wiles of the enemy. Baal, as was described in the last chapter, desires to wed himself to us in order to destroy our covenant destiny with God. But we are not and were never intended to be wedded to anyone except the Lord our God. Jesus Christ is our groom. He is our husband. The ancient foe continues to seek new ways to devour, distract, destroy and deceive the people of God.

Journey for a moment back to Nehemiah 2:20. As Nehemiah carries out the gatekeeping task of rebuilding the walls and gates of Jerusalem, we were first introduced to Sanballat, Tobiah and their cronies. They laughed at Nehemiah's cause and Nehemiah answered: "The God of heaven Himself will prosper us; therefore, we His servants will arise and build, but you have no heritage or right or memorial in Jerusalem."

We were reminded in 2 Corinthians 2:11 (Amplified) "to keep Satan from getting the advantage over us; for we are not ignorant of his wiles and intentions." We discovered in Chapter 12 that the enemy has many schemes and devises. We found that the ancient foe – Satan and especially Baal will persist in trying to defeat us and our destinies in God. Through Sanballat and Tobiah we uncovered the first of several schemes that were thrown at Nehemiah. Sanballat and Tobiah—driven by jealousy and rage—mocked the Jews. Nehemiah responded with (1) prayer, (2) leaving vengeance against his enemies up to God and (3) continuing to build.

## THE PLOT THICKENS

Now it happened, when Sanballat, Tobiah, the Arabs, the Ammonites, and the Ashdodites heard that the walls of Jerusalem were being restored and the gaps were beginning to be closed, that they became very angry, and all of them conspired together to come and attack Jerusalem and create confusion. (Nehemiah 4:7-8)

Notice how the size of the enemy has increased. In the last attack, it was only Sanballat and Tobiah. Then the Arabs (from Arabia to the southeast), the Ammonites (to the east) and the Ashdodites (the old Philistines to the southwest) joined them. The war is always bigger than we think. We may see the small picture, but Satan is aware of the eternal consequences even of our seemingly small assignments. The enemy was being threatened at a higher level. Why? Because…the walls were being restored and the gaps (breaches) were beginning to be closed.

The agents of Baal became angry. It was a hot burning anger based on jealousy. And their jealous anger lead the enemy to conspire (to be physically and mentally knit together), to carry out a frontal attack on the city in order to create confusion. Mocking and jeering alone had not produced results. They sought to destroy the city and those who tried to rebuild it.

## NEHEMIAH'S RESPONSE - SET A WATCH

Nevertheless, we made our prayer to our God, and because of them we set a watch against them day and night. (Nehemiah 4:9)

Again, Nehemiah returned to the heart of the issue – prayer. He is betrothed to the Lord. He and the people are married to the Lord and out of that relationship; he prayed and established a watch. They literally set guards in place to diligently watch for the enemy. But even with prayer and the watch—the people were unsettled with fear.

Then Judah said, "The strength of the laborers is failing, and there is so much rubbish that we are not able to build the wall." It is true—we don't have strength and there is too much work to do. And our adversaries said, "They will neither know nor see anything, till we come into their midst and kill them and cause the work to cease." They won't know what hit them. This conversation hints at the presence of spies. So, it was, when the Jews who dwelt near them came, that they told us ten times, "From whatever place you turn, they will be upon us." Wherever we turn—the enemy is upon us. (Nehemiah 4:10-12, comments mine).

The battle is getting fierce but notice that Nehemiah did not "belittle the people" nor did he "shame them." He continued to strategize **out of his communion with God.**

Therefore, I positioned men behind the lower parts of the wall, at the openings; and I set the people according to their families, with their swords, their spears, and their bows. And I looked, and arose and said to the nobles, to the leaders, and to the rest of the people, "Do not be afraid of them. Remember the Lord, great and awesome, and fight for your brethren, your sons, your daughters, your wives, and your houses" (Nehemiah 4:13-14).

He positioned men at the low points in the wall. He placed them at the openings (the gaps) in the walls. This is a powerful image of intercession – taking up a position on behalf of other people and your city. He gave the people weapons and stationed them according to family on the high places. He placed them at the gaps and up on the wall (literally exposed to the sun). He placed families out before the enemy. You've got to be kidding! Isn't this the place for professional warriors? Surely you are not going to use the common people to fight?

He told them to look to their great and awesome God and to fight. Satan's first plot was strictly "mental." He was trying to persuade them by questioning their ability. This second plot is a full-frontal attack. We must stand firm in our position and be prepared to fight. And notice the response by the enemy.

And it happened, when our enemies heard that it was known to us, and that God had brought their plot to nothing, that all of us returned to the wall, everyone to his work (Nehemiah 4:15).

The battle was won but the people must stay prepared.

Be sober, be vigilant; because your adversary the devil walks about like a roaring lion, seeking whom he may devour. Resist him, steadfast in the faith, knowing that the same sufferings are experienced by your brotherhood in the world. But may the God of all grace, who called us to His eternal glory by Christ Jesus, after you have suffered a while, perfect, establish, strengthen, and settle you. To Him be the glory and the dominion forever and ever. Amen. (1 Peter 5:8-11).

As you read the next few verses of Nehemiah 4 you discover that half of the people worked and the other half held spears. The leaders took position behind them and covered them. They encouraged them. They supported them. Gone are the days of old church ministry when the pastor would find all the battles and the people would sometimes stand him or her. The Lord is sending out gatekeepers – a kingdom of priests – made up of common everyday people – homemakers, corporate executives, plumbers, students and laborers. He places leaders behind them to equip them for ministry and to encourage them to fight the good fight.

Those on the wall worked with one hand and had a weapon in the other. Everyone had a sword girded to his side. As I read this I am reminded of our trips to Israel. The Israeli soldiers we saw on "holiday" were still required to carry their weapons. A trumpet was in place to communicate with the network of people. The trumpet was a constant reminder of our call to prayer and war. The work continued day and night—the battle is ongoing. The people had poised their hearts and minds to hear God as he called them to pray—to battle—to build.

## ANOTHER PLOT UNFOLDS–DISSENSION IN THE RANKS

There is now dissension in the ranks. Read the story from <u>The Message</u>.

A great protest was mounted by the people, including the wives, against their fellow Jews. Some said, "We have big families, and we need food just to survive." Others said, "We're having to mortgage our fields and vineyards and homes to get enough grain to keep from starving." And others said, "We're having to borrow money to pay the royal tax on our fields and vineyards. Look: We're the same flesh and blood as our brothers here; our children are just as good as theirs. Yet here we are having to sell our children off as slaves — some of our daughters have already been sold — and we can't do anything about it because our fields and vineyards are owned by somebody else." I (Nehemiah) got really angry when I heard their protest and complaints. After thinking it over, I called the nobles and officials on the carpet. I said, "Each one of you is gouging his brother." Then I called a big meeting to deal with them. I told them,

"We did everything we could to buy back our Jewish brothers who had to sell themselves as slaves to foreigners. And now you're selling these same brothers back into debt slavery! Does that mean that we have to buy them back again?" They said nothing. What could they say? "What you're doing is wrong. **Is there no fear of God left in you? Don't you care what the nations around here, our enemies, think of you?** "I and my brothers and the people working for me have also loaned them money. But this gouging them with interest has to stop. Give them back their foreclosed fields, vineyards, olive groves, and homes right now. And forgive your claims on their money, grain, new wine, and olive oil." They said, "We'll give it all back. We won't make any more demands on them. We'll do everything you say." Then I called the priests together and made them promise to keep their word. Then I emptied my pockets, turning them inside out, and said, "So may God empty the pockets and house of everyone who doesn't keep this promise — turned inside out and emptied." Everyone gave a wholehearted "Yes, we'll do it!" and praised GOD. And the people did what they promised. (Nehemiah 5:1-13, emphasis mine)

The chapter finishes with Nehemiah declaring what has been the heart of the leadership from the beginning. Their desire has been to fear God. The enemy (in an unseen fashion) attacked the people—but once again they were led back to the heart of God. "Remember in my favor, O my God, everything I've done for these people" (Nehemiah 5:19).

## THE FULLNESS OF DECEPTION
At the beginning of Nehemiah 6 we once again we hear about Sanballat and Tobiah—the persistence of our enemy.

Now it happened when Sanballat, Tobiah, Geshem the Arab, and the rest of our enemies heard that I had rebuilt the wall, and that there were no breaks left in it (though at that time I had not hung the doors in the gates), that Sanballat and Geshem sent to me, saying, "Come, let us meet together among the villages in the plain of Ono." But they thought to do me harm. (Nehemiah 6:1, 2)

Come—let us meet together. The greatest scheme of the enemy is compromise. Let's talk about this—there must be something we can do to work out our differences. It's sounds good—but in God's realm there is no compromising with the enemy. NOTE: I'm not talking here about two friends, spouses, co-workers or such that are working out differences of opinion. We are talking about compromising the kingdom.

So, I sent messengers to them, saying, "I am doing a great work, so that I cannot come down. Why should the work cease while I leave it and go down to you?" But they sent me this message four times, and I answered them in the same manner. (Nehemiah 6:3,4)

Nehemiah won't compromise. He won't waste his time on talking with the enemy. We live in a world defined by political correctness, compromise and tolerance. As I stated earlier, these words are not always bad when we are trying to work wounded relationships. But as we deal with the enemy of our souls – these are deadly. The enemy is persistent. The enemy wants nothing more than to kill, steal and destroy. You don't compromise with evil. You don't arrange deals or trades with the enemy or any of his tactics.

I remember a weekend I was serving on a weekend prayer team. As the pastor on the team I was there to give them spiritual direction. We were praying for a group of people going through an intense spiritual weekend of their own. At one point, we were praying for one of the leaders speaking at the other retreat. He was very sick. We were praying for his healing when one of my team members declared. This person cannot be sick. If anyone needs to be sick – let it be me. I will take their sickness and I give them my health. To say the least I jumped on that immediately. We do not trade with the enemy. We make no deals with the enemy.

Then Sanballat sent his servant to me as before, the fifth time, with an open letter in his hand. In it was written: "It is reported among the nations, and Geshem says, that you and the Jews plan to rebel; therefore, according to these rumors, you are rebuilding the wall, that you may be their king. And you have also appointed prophets to proclaim concerning you at Jerusalem, saying, "There is a king in Judah!" Now these matters will be reported to the king. So, come, therefore, and let us consult together. (Nehemiah 6:6, 7)

Sanballat cried out, "It is reported—you are intolerant, you are hard headed, you are a fundamentalist, you are a rebel. You are going to be reported." Isn't it intriguing that in the midst of deception the enemy is going to serve notice to the king. This king is the one who trusted and sent Nehemiah. The goal is not truth—but defeat.

Then I sent to him, saying, "No such things as you say are being done, but you invent them in your own heart." For they all were trying to make us afraid, saying, "Their hands will be weakened in the work, and it will not be done." Now therefore, O God, strengthen my hands. (Nehemiah 6:8, 9)

Nehemiah perceived the problem and once again went to God. We now reach the final ploy.

Afterward I came to the house of Shemaiah the son of Delaiah, the son of Mehetabel, who was a secret informer; and he said, "Let us meet together in the house of God, within the temple, and let us close the doors of the temple, for they are coming to kill you; indeed, at night they will come to kill you." And I said, "Should such a man as I flee? And who is there such as I who would go into the temple to save his life? I will not go in!" Then I perceived that God had not sent him at all, but that he pronounced this prophecy against me because Tobiah and Sanballat had hired him. For this reason, he was hired, that I should be afraid and act that way and sin, so that they might have cause for an evil report, that they might reproach me. My God, remember Tobiah and Sanballat, according to these their works, and the prophetess Noadiah and the rest of the prophets who would have made me afraid. (Nehemiah 6:10-14).

Let's go to the temple and close the doors—secrecy and deception. Nehemiah because of a close intimate and communing relationship with God perceived the deception. He once again turned his enemies over to God.

## THE WALL COMPLETED
So, the wall was finished on the twenty-fifth day of Elul, in fifty-two days. And it happened, when all our enemies heard of it, and all the nations

around us saw these things, that they were very disheartened in their own eyes; **for they perceived that this work was done by our God.** (Nehemiah 6:15, 16, emphasis mine).

The wall was completed but the job was not done. Let's jump ahead in Nehemiah and read from Nehemiah 13.

"On that day, they read from the Book of Moses in the hearing of the people, and in it was found written that no Ammonite or Moabite should ever come into the assembly of God, because they had not met the children of Israel with bread and water, but hired Balaam against them to curse them. However, our God turned the curse into a blessing. So, it was, when they had heard the Law, that they separated all the mixed multitude from Israel" (Nehemiah 13:1-3).

The walls have been completed. The people have been encouraged. The city has been brought back into alignment. But wait! After reading the Book of Moses, Nehemiah was reminded (in the Book of Numbers) that Balaam had been hired by Balak (the strategy of Baal) of Moab to curse and destroy the covenant people of Israel. It was not to be tolerated. And yet Eliashib in conspiracy with Tobiah of Moab had garnered control of the temple treasury. Remember from the description of Baal in the last chapter that Baal-hamon, one of Baal's names, means "the lord of wealth or abundance." He is the principality warring against the great transfer of wealth to the church. We are to war against this spirit in order to see our inheritance released. Nehemiah had a decision to make. Notice his response.

"Now before this, Eliashib the priest, having authority over the storerooms of the house of our God, was allied with Tobiah. And he had prepared for him a large room, where previously they had stored the grain offerings, the frankincense, the articles, the tithes of grain, the new wine and oil, which were commanded to be given to the Levites and singers and gatekeepers, and the offerings for the priests. But during all this I was not in Jerusalem, for in the thirty-second year of Artaxerxes king of Babylon I had returned to the king. Then after certain days I obtained leave from the king, and I came to Jerusalem and discovered the evil that Eliashib had done for Tobiah, in preparing a room for him in the courts of the house of God. And it grieved me bitterly; therefore, I threw all the household goods of Tobiah out of the room. Then I commanded them to cleanse the rooms; and I brought back into them the articles of the house of God, with the grain offering and the frankincense" (Nehemiah 13:4-9).

Up until the very last moment the enemy was seeking to steal, kill and destroy. The enemy is persistent. He will not quit until this very day.

So, after the pattern of Nehemiah, in our role as gatekeepers, we gathered on the hills of Olney and once again declared that we will not be married to any other husband than our Lord.[58] Take a moment to examine your own life. Are their areas that you have "married" Baal? Are you depending on the world system to bring you provision? Are you desiring, craving and acting upon sexual issues such as internet pornography, perversion, homosexuality or unfaithfulness? Are you making covenant with God and the world – with God and Mammon? Are you passing on a godly heritage to the next generation or are you cutting them off physically and spiritually?

"And it shall be, in that day," says the LORD, that you will call Me 'My Husband,' and no longer call Me 'My Master,' for I will take from her mouth the names of the Baals, and they shall be remembered by their name no more. In that day, I will make a covenant for them with the beasts of the field, with the birds of the air, and with the creeping things of the ground. Bow and sword of battle I will shatter from the earth, to make them lie down safely. "I will betroth you to Me forever; yes, I will betroth you to Me in righteousness and justice, in lovingkindness and mercy; I will betroth you to Me in faithfulness, and you shall know the LORD" (Hosea 2:16-20).

## LET US PRAY

Lord, You have betrothed Yourself to me. I am Yours and You are mine. I ask today that You will examine me with Your grace and mercy-filled eyes and determine if there is anything in me that longs for another husband. Lord, of all those things I repent. I lay them down at Your feet. I decree a divorce from Baal. I no longer am married to him. Open my eyes to see the destiny that You have laid out before me. Let me rise up and build. Let me grasp my purpose in You. Draw me into relationship with my brothers and sisters in Your kingdom and let us together invite You to fully come. You have vanquished the enemy. You will bring forth the fullness of Your glory. Amen.

# 14

## At the Threshold

*"When Israel went out of Egypt, the house of Jacob from a people of strange language, Judah became His sanctuary, and Israel His dominion"*

*(Psalm 114:1, 2).*

Throughout the first half of the year 2006 the Lord had been speaking clearly to our congregation that He had indeed established us as gatekeepers of our city and region and that He was about to thrust us through the gate. He was going to us as instruments for releasing His blessing and apostolic authority into the area. At the beginning of the year the Lord had delivered to our congregation Psalm 114 as a point of reference for the entire year. It is Psalm 114.

When Israel went out of Egypt,
The house of Jacob from a people of strange language,
Judah became His sanctuary,
And Israel His dominion.
The sea saw it and fled;
Jordan turned back.

The mountains skipped like rams,
The little hills like lambs.
What ails you, O sea, that you fled?
O Jordan, that you turned back?
O mountains, that you skipped like rams?
O little hills, like lambs?
Tremble, O earth, at the presence of the Lord,
At the presence of the God of Jacob,
Who turned the rock into a pool of water,
The flint into a fountain of waters.

The Lord declared that we would become His sanctuary (a place of intimacy) and a place of His dominion (apostolic authority). We have embraced this word and are witnessing its fulfillment. In July 2006, our family prepared for my son's wedding. Beverly McIntyre, a good friend of our family, came to help with the decorations. Beverly is the founder and director of Change Point Ministries in Arizona.[59] I asked her to bring the Sunday morning message to our congregation. She was totally unaware of the Lord's previous words to us regarding gates and gatekeepers. It was obviously a "word in season" from our Lord. The following is an adapted and edited version of the sermon she preached on July 23, 2006.

## THE GATE

When the Word of God speaks of a gate it is not the same kind of gate we know in the Western Culture. A gate is an opening in a wall or "walled city" that keeps people in or out. To enter in or go out you must go to the gate. At every gate, there are guards that stand on duty to make sure only those who are supposed to leave or enter can have access to the gate.

At the wall were always guards that stood watch over the gates. Many things happened at the gates. It was at the gates that the men would go to establish the government. It was at the gate that law was established. In the Book of Esther, her cousin Mordecai went to the gate with the noble men of the community, and according to Proverbs 1:21, Wisdom makes her speech at the gate of the city. So, a gate is a place of prominence and a place where entry is a most desirable thing.

## GATES ARE IMPORTANT IN THE BIBLE AND THEY ARE IMPORTANT TO THE BODY OF CHRIST.

"I will surely gather all of you, O Jacob; I will surely bring together the remnant of Israel. I will bring them together like sheep in a pen, like a flock in its pasture; the place will throng with people. One who breaks open the way will go up before them; they will break through the gate and go out. Their king will pass through before them, the Lord at their head" (Micah 2: 12, 13).

I believe the Body of Christ is on the brink of something. It is not another revival. It is not another healing era. It is a complete transformation of the Body of Christ. It is the people of God learning to take the land that the enemy has held on to. It is the place where the promises of God dwell. It is you and I going right into the places that have held us captive and demanding the gate open!

## THE ONE WHO BREAKS OPEN

The One who breaks open the way has gone up before us, and He is calling us to come now and break through the gate. God has opened the gate to us but many of us have a problem walking through it. I don't believe that it is the gate that is the problem. The problem lies at the threshold. The enemy stops us at the threshold.

God has been speaking to me through Nehemiah and through various revelations about gates and what God is doing about gates right now in the Body of Christ. We are standing in that place where God is saying, "I want you to come, and I am going to open the gate." There have been many gates in our life that have not been opened. There are gates that all of us have tried to open.

When the Children of Israel went into the Promised Land, they had to go in city by city and take the land. When they would go into a city, they would have to get through the gate to take the city. It was a difficult thing to get through the gate that led to the land God had promised.

Right now, I believe that the Body of Christ is standing at many gates that have looked closed. We have been knocking and knocking, and we have been saying, "When will it open? Why won't it open? What is going on? Why can't I see this happen?" There are some things in our life that we have quit praying about, that we don't talk about any more. We have given up because the gate didn't open. We stood at the threshold, and the gate didn't open.

We know from Micah 2:3 that God, the Breaker, goes before us and breaks open the way, but what compels Him to open the gate?

## IT TAKES FAITH

It takes faith to open the gate that stands in front of you. It takes a life of integrity. Walking out our faith in fear and trembling...not fear of the enemy but having enough fear of God to walk in discipline and obedience to him.

I heard John Bevere[60] recount a conversation that he had with a man who had been in the ministry that had fallen into a life of sin. He asked the man when he stopped loving the Lord. The man looked at him and said, he had never stopped loving the Lord, he just never had the feared the Lord! To walk with God and go through the places that will bring us to those precious promises He has so faithfully given us we must fear Him more than man or more than the enemy. The gates are open but it is at the threshold that we get hung up.

## THE GATE HAS TO BE OPENED BY GOD

The gate has to be opened by God. What is the gate that stands in front of you? Maybe it's the Gate of Healing. Maybe you need healing in your body, and you say, "Lord, I'm tired of asking You. That is a heavy gate. You've stood at that gate, and you've knocked and you've pounded and you've said, "Let me in!" And you don't know how to get in.

Maybe it's financial. You've believed God and believed God and believed God, and it's worse. You've stood at that gate. God says I'm calling my people right now into a place of faith and obedience. I'm calling you into a new level of faith, a new level of obedience. The next movement of God will take responsibility on our part. He says, "I have a gate that stands before you. The enemy has kept it closed. The enemy has been the watchman on that wall. The enemy has said, 'Keep them out.'"

If the enemy can keep us defeated he doesn't care what we do. When we are faced with the decision of accepting Jesus as our Lord and Savior we are standing in front of the very gate of Heaven. This gate is open to us when the Holy Spirit comes to convict us of our sin. This is the place of sacrifice of our hearts. This is where we come through the Blood of Jesus for our salvation. The enemy can't go through the Blood but he can stand outside the gate. He places his demons there to guard the threshold to keep us from walking through that gate.

## AT THE THRESHOLD

According to Barbara Yoder in her book, "The Breaker Anointing" the warfare for our walk takes place at the threshold. She writes:

"...There are two words for "threshold" in Hebrew. These words reveal that there is warfare at the gates and warfare over the threshold. One of the Hebrew words is caph. It is the word used for "door (post)," "gate," "post" and "threshold." Caph is from caphaph, a primitive root that means "to snatch away or terminate." The second word used for threshold in Hebrew is miphtan, which is from pethen, an unused root meaning "to twist as a snake." It is pronounced much like "python" and is probably where the name of the snake was derived. Pythons destroy their prey by wrapping their bodies around them and suffocating them."[61]

Think of this in light of just coming to the Lord for forgiveness of sin. When the Holy Spirit comes to convict us of our sin the enemy stands just outside the gate before we can cross into the gate area and through the Blood to snatch us away from the godly conviction that is upon us. He comes with lies like: "You're not good enough to be forgiven." "You can't stop doing that, you'll just do it again and God is sick of hearing you." "You've never measured up and you never will measure up." Have you ever heard messages like this? When you begin to hear words of condemnation know that you must be standing at a gate and God is just on the other side waiting to take you through.

The threshold is an entrance where something in your life kicks into action. It's where that thing that has been lying dormant or that thing that you have never seen come to pass begins to kick into action because you have walked in faith and obedience.

Barbara Yoder puts it this way in her book, "The Breaker Anointing",

"...The threshold is where something kicks into action. It is the minimal amount of something needed to induce a corresponding action. For instance, we refer to the threshold of pain, threshold of new discovery and threshold of a door."

"...it (threshold) represents the place of ultimate risk-risking total loss. It is the place of greatest vulnerability yet it is also the place from which we must leap if we are to get to the other side." It is a place of total loss. It is a place of greatest vulnerability, yet it is a place from which we must leap if we are going to the other side – the place where faith must arise. Faith-filled people of God take bold action, which opens the gate and releases spiritual power" (emphasis added).[62]

## TWO PRINCIPALITIES – FEAR AND PYTHON

At the threshold of the gate there are two principalities that stand against us. They are the "caph" that comes to snatch away or terminate our going through. This spirit rules through fear. I have felt that spirit breathing on me so many times in my life at the point of making a decision or coming into a new place in the Lord. Whenever we stand at a place of transition the devil will try to stop us.

The enemy comes to snatch us away from what God has called us to. If he can't get us to run in the face of opposition then he comes in with another strategy. He begins to twist the truth of God. He allows us to believe that God is angry that there are no real open doors for us. He is there to hinder us in every way from going forward into the gate that stands open to us.

When he comes to twist he comes to destroy the "Word of God" in our life. That word can come through the written word that God spoke in a moment of rhema to us or through a prophetic word. Psalms 24:7 and 8 says "Lift up your heads, O you gates; be lifted up, you ancient doors, that the King of glory may come in. Who is this King of glory? The Lord strong and mighty, the Lord mighty in battle."

In Bible times when someone was approaching the gate the watchman would shout out who was coming and shout out if the gate should be opened. God is asking us now "Will you shout out to that situation in your life? Will you shout out to that situation and will you say, 'Open up, O ye gates that the king of glory may come in."

## SHOUT OUT AT THE THRESHOLD

At the writing of this I am facing a gate of my own. I founded Change Point, a ministry that brings the prophetic ministry into some of the worst places in the world. During the Bosnian war, prior to the United States getting involved or the news informing us of the situation there I went 5 times and successfully ministered to the women who had been victims of that war in some of the worst atrocities I had ever known. This has been a great 10 years with God taking us all over the world.

My husband for years and years has had words spoken over him that he has anointing for wealth, that he has anointing for prosperity. He will get words that say he will be like a watered garden and to enlarge the stakes of his tents because the Lord is enlarging his territory. Every time we get to that place where we really start to believe God, something happens and we shrink back.

In the past 10 years, although there has been enough money to go on our "mission trips," we have not had enough to pay salaries. Consequently, I have decorated homes for women on the side. The decorating has brought in enough to meet my personal needs but on the down side, it keeps me very busy with the things that I know God has not called me to do. The enemy came to me in the middle of the night one night not long ago about my ministry and about our finances. He said, "This time you are not going to make it. Financially, you are not going to have anything. I am going to keep stealing the finances from the ministry. I'm going to steal the finances from you personally, and you are not going to make it."

I got up and went into the living room and all night long this is what I said to the enemy, "Enemy, I will fight you at the threshold of the gate. I will fight you at the threshold of this gate. I will fight you at the threshold of this gate because the blood of Jesus covers my life. The blood of Jesus is there, and this time I will walk through this gate."

It was after this huge battle with the enemy during the night that my husband got an opportunity for a job with potential to bring in the finances that have been spoken over him for so many years. We have relocated to another state. Not only do I live in another state where I know few people but my house sits in the country on a hill all alone.[63] I am 25 minutes from the closest grocery store. My life has drastically changed. We don't understand why we made this move but both of us feel a great peace about it and feel that this is a part of the fulfillment of what God has spoken over him for many years. I had to lay down the decorating. Since I have not been doing the decorating jobs I am accustomed to doing I am battling going through this gate that God has opened for me. My new home is in the perfect place to seek Him, to spend time with Him, to write and draw closer to Him.[64] This is something that I have prayed for, "time". Now, the enemy is waking me up at night gripping me with fear that I better get some decorating jobs to sustain myself financially. Not only that, he is coming trying to twist every word the Lord has ever spoken to me.

I asked the Lord to speak to me again and in His great faithfulness He has continued to speak that He is with me in all my circumstances. We have to learn to live according to His word. We have to learn to shout at the gate when the enemy is stopping us at the threshold and shout to the gate, "Open up O you gate that the King of glory may come in!"

Whenever you receive a prophetic word the enemy comes and places a watchman over that prophetic word to keep you from ever walking into it. God speaks to us that everything is going to be just as He says and then He speaks again and then He speaks again in another way and He does this so we will remember when we are in the thick of the battle at the threshold that God is with us and we can take this land.

He puts a watchman at the gate where we received a prophetic word of our destiny and he guards it saying to his demon watchmen, "Keep them from walking into that place. When they get to the threshold of that destiny, of that gate, stop them." See, the enemy watches over those thresholds.

## AT THE BRINK

Another word for threshold is "brink." It's a moving toward a new territory. You know when Moses got to the very "brink" of the river, he stopped. He didn't know what to do. The enemy was crowding from behind. They were running. They were after them. Moses stood at that river. He was at the "brink" of disaster. He was at the brink of death. He was at the brink any way he turned. He was at the brink of death. When he stood at that river he had to make a decision. He had to go forward or he had to go backward. The Lord spoke to Moses and said, "Go forward." The enemy said, "You cannot cross this river." But Moses put his foot in the river, and the river dried up, and the Children of Israel walked across the river.

The same thing is happening to us right now. We are on the "brink" of a great and mighty transition into our very destiny and the enemy is watching as we come to the place of no return and he is standing there to keep us from going forward.

The same thing happened with Joshua when it was time to go into the Promised Land. The Lord said, "Send the priests to take the ark into the middle of the river." When Joshua stood at the brink of that river, he had to make a choice. See, we stand at the brink, and we say, "I can't do it" because at the brink of any new territory is where the enemy stands guard. And what he stands guard to do is to scare you to death. He stands guard to stop you.

## THE BIGGEST BATTLE IS AT THE THRESHOLD.

Once you get inside the gate, on the other side, all of a sudden you have faith to believe. You believe for it. Before you gave your heart to Jesus, you couldn't even imagine being a Christian. You couldn't even imagine how anyone could live like that. Before I became a Christian, I thought, "Why do people want to go to church? It is the most boring thing in the world to me. Why? Why would anybody want to do that? I could not live that life. But, once I crossed that threshold into salvation, then all of a sudden God changed the desires of my heart and the things that I once hated, I loved and the things that I once loved, I now hated. I wanted to be in church. I wanted to do the things God wanted me to do. It is the same with everything that we walk through.

There are so many times in our lives that the enemy comes like a python to squeeze the life out of us and to say to us, "You're not going to make it. This time you are going to die. This time everything is going to fail. This time you are going under. This time God is not going to show up. This time it is not going to be like it was before when you were a young Christian and you could believe Him. This time it's all lost."

God says, "Look, the winter is past. Come with Me on the other side because the Breaker Anointing has gone before you. The Breaker Anointing has gone before you into that gate, and it has opened wide the gate." It is at the threshold that we have to overcome. That thing tries to take our breath, which sustains our life. The very breath of God sustains our life. God is there to breathe prophetic breath in to us, which imparts life to us.

## THERE IS ALWAYS A CRISIS RELATED TO THE PROPHETIC WORD AT THE GATE.

Whenever you get a prophetic word, whenever someone gives a prophetic word over you or God speaks to you out of the Word and you know that you know that you know that God spoke to you – let me tell you – when you get to the gate of that thing, there is going to be a battle. There will be a crisis at the gate. **It is at the threshold that we make the decision – I am going through or I am not going to go through**.

The enemy comes to take that prophetic vision. The Word says that without a vision the people perish.[65] Do you know that **that means that without prophetic vision we perish**? I have to know what God means in my life. It's good to know what He means in your life, but I need to know what He means in my life. What is He going to do in my life? What is His vision for me? Without knowing His vision for me, I will perish. So, the prophetic word comes and God discloses His prophetic vision over me. Prophetic ministry is so important. Without prophetic ministry, the church will perish. We will walk blindly into the future not knowing the plans God has for us. We will not know how to prepare for our destiny.

Prophecy is hand-in-hand with prayer. As we pray, we receive. God doesn't want us to just to talk to Him. He wants to talk back to us. When He comes and speaks to us, the enemy comes and says, "It's not going to happen." Sometimes we believe the word for a few days. Have you ever just listened to your word and listened to what God has spoken to you for a few days and you listen and listen and after a few days you put it away and three weeks later you're facing a trial, and it's concerning that word, and you forget you even got it. The enemy comes to snatch that word away from us and squeeze the life out of us. He comes to take that prophetic revelation from us.

God is saying to us, "You go back to those places where you received the word of the Lord. Go back and look at those places where you received the word of the Lord, and when you look at those places, take that prophetic word and say to the gate, "Open up, You Gate, that the King of Glory may come in. Open up this gate inside of me."

## THE RIGHT AND LEFT HAND

Our hearts were pumping with excitement and victory as Beverly preached that Sunday. The Lord had revealed to us the purpose of the gates. He had revealed to us the power of His kingdom being released through us as we declare the things discovered and purposed in His heart. Many of us; however, felt that we had become stranded in the threshold because of the plots and schemes of the enemy. We had been halted by fear and strangled by the python as we stood on the brink of a great adventure.

Almost out of context, near the end of the message Beverly spoke about the right and left hand. She shared with us that the right hand or right side of the body is symbolic of our authority – it speaks of the prophetic word of God. The left side is symbolic of the plans and purposes of God in your life. It relates to our destiny.

## GOD DEALT WITH OUR DESTINY!

During that next week, I had developed a severe pain in my left shoulder. Three of the members of the church had had severe problems with their eyes. One of those persons was an elder and it was his left eye that was the culprit. I researched more and discovered that the two other elders had "left-side issues" as well. As a matter of fact, several of the members testified the same thing – something on the left side of their body was out of alignment. The Lord, through our prayers, gave us discernment and revelation. He told us that we were standing at the gates and that His authority needed to be released through us, but our destiny (left side) was being strangled by Python. The next Sunday the elders and I stood before the congregation and prophetically with a sword and the Word of God "caught off" the work of Python from each member. We also cut off the spirit of fear that was freezing us into inactivity.

Over the next four months the Lord marvelously revealed five more spirits that He was dealing with in our midst. In times of worship, in our time of partaking of the Lord's supper and in our times of prophetic intercession and prayer the Lord exposed the spirit of religion which was desiring to cancel out our freedom in the Spirit, the spirit of poverty which was destroying the blessedness of giving and exchanging it with a fear of lack, the spirit of pride which was seeking to establish independence and therefore destroying unity in the body of Christ, the spirit of hopelessness which was causing us to focus on loss and trauma rather than God, and finally the spirit of unbelief which was keeping us from confidently grasping the Word of God and His promises and obediently stepping through the gate.

As I personally and prophetically stepped through the gate and into the new place the pain in my shoulder, which had lasted for over four months, disappeared. We are moving in our destiny. You are to move in yours! Stand up in faith. Grasp God's promises. As a prophetic act, even as you read this book, cut off the restricting and strangling python spirit in the name of Jesus. Cut off fear. Cut off pride and poverty. Cut off hopelessness. In the midst of loss and trauma, step into the hope and joy of God. Cut off religion and all of its stifling traditions. I attended a prayer meeting at Glory of Zion Ministries in Denton, Texas and Pastor Robert Heidler shared a testimony of his trip to the prayer meeting that very morning. He was on a two-lane road which was stacked up with traffic. It should have been going 45 miles an hour but it was crawling at 30 or less. The problem was the truck immediately in front of Robert. It was a bread truck and nobody could get by. The Lord drew Robert's attention to the logo on the truck. It read "LOADED WITH TRADITION." That is the spirit of religion. Cut off its ability to stall or stop your growth and movement in the Spirit.

And finally – cut off the spirit of unbelief. Lift up your head O gate and behold the Lord God Almighty. He is enthroned as King. He will fulfill His word over your life, family, ministry and city. Lift up your head O gate and invite the King to come in. Believe in Him and step over the threshold into the fullness of His kingdom. Step over the threshold into that place where He has promised to move through you in order to transform this world with His authority.

On the last Sunday of October 2006, the Lord spoke a word to me and to our congregation. It was seven years (a time of completion) since He had revealed the word about kings and priests which I recorded in my book, Return of the Priests. Turn with me to the next chapter for that prophetic word given on October 29, 2006 is also meant for you!

# 15

## Set In Place

*"Then it was, when the wall was built and I had hung the doors, when the gatekeepers, the singers, and the Levites had been appointed..."*

(NEHEMIAH 7:1).

### A WORD FROM THE LORD

Stand firm and see the salvation of your God! Do not waver! Do not fret! You are in a new place. A new Reformation is moving in your midst."

The Lord gave me this word on October 29, 2006. As He spoke I remembered that on Sunday, October 31, 1999 I had preached a message entitled "The Unfinished Task." It pertained to the Reformation started by Martin Luther. It was during that message and through other prophetic words and dreams that the Lord began to reveal to me the heart of the message on kings and priests that I eventually recorded in my book, Return of the Priests. But His word to me continued...

"You now begin the eighth year – the year of new beginnings. The age of Melchizedek begins."

The Lord made it clear to me that we were in a new place. He further clarified for us that we had moved through the transition. We had crossed the threshold. And it was **not** our act of walking that brought us to this new place but His divine act of lifting us up out of one place and putting us into another. And in this new place He has declared and decreed to us that we will now move in His full apostolic authority.

Almost twenty years ago, when I was serving in another church, we lived in a small community on the outskirts of Abilene, Texas. We have always had pets – mostly cats. One cat that belonged to us (no, that's not right. Cats don't belong to us, we belong to them) was named Smokie. She was a real mouser. She lived both indoors and outdoors. When she was outside she faithfully would catch mice and other small rodents and deliver them to our front porch (and sometimes we saw nothing but fur and other remains scattered on the lawn). One afternoon as my wife Kay was preparing supper she opened the cabinets above the stove and shrieked when she saw a mouse scurrying in the cabinet. I arrived on the scene with a big stick and a determined purpose to destroy the enemy. My acts though proved futile not fatal. The mouse continually outmaneuvered me. I was thinking of putting out a trap when Smokie walked by my feet. Almost without thinking I lifted her up by the nap of the neck, placed her in the cabinet and closed the door.

The next few moments were filled with sounds of items being pushed over in the cabinet but the sounds lasted only seconds. Quietness filled the kitchen. I heard a small scratch at the cabinet and carefully opened it. There in all her pride was Smokie and the enemy was firmed caught in her teeth. I once again lifted her up and out of the cabinet – mouse and all – and placed her outside. You know the rest of the story.

The memory of Smokie's adventure filled my heart as the Lord told us that He had lifted us into a new place to carry out His kingdom authority. The season for the enemy to have the upper hand in our city is nearing an end. God has called and released His gatekeepers and gates into strategic places. By the way, in case you forget what your strategic place is – take a look at where you are right now! God has positioned us to be His ambassadors, priests, warriors and kings in homes, businesses, schools, government positions, churches, neighborhoods, cities, states, and nations. He has and is continuing to equip us to do the work of ministry.

"And He Himself gave some to be apostles, some prophets, some evangelists, and some pastors and teachers, for the equipping of the saints **for the work of ministry**, for the edifying of the body of Christ, **till we all come to the unity of the faith** and of **the knowledge of the Son of God**, to a perfect man, **to the measure of the stature of the fullness of Christ**; that we should no longer be children, tossed to and fro and carried about with every wind of doctrine, by the trickery of men, in the cunning craftiness of deceitful plotting, but, speaking the truth in love, may grow up in all things into Him who is the head – Christ – from whom the whole body, joined and knit together by what every joint supplies, according to the effective working by which every part does its share, causes growth of the body for the edifying of itself in love" (Ephesians 4:11-16, emphasis mine).

He has released us to do kingdom ministry. Like Nehemiah He will equip us to transform the city into His glory. How? He has made us as gates which will stand open and ready to allow the fullness of God and all His majesty, glory, light, life and power to flow though us into the places of our habitation. The gates of hell will not prevail against the gates of God's church and kingdom.

In the Introduction of this book I was sharing the vision the Lord had given. I quote the end of that vision again.

"We walked on. It became darker and darker if it could possibly become darker. Then I saw a ray of light. It was like a gem or diamond with an iridescent glow – a very light iridescent glow just hanging out there. I couldn't really see anything around it except that the Lord was holding it.

I said, "What is this, Lord?"

And He said, "This is My heart. I want you to take it."

As I took it into my hands, I felt warmth and light coursing through me and over me. And I said, "Lord, Your love – It is overwhelming!"

Then light began to be released to everything around me. Now I was seeing the city again, but now the city was completely restored. It had new streets, new buildings -- The buildings were all polished and beautiful. I knew that it wasn't Heaven. It literally was the city. Whether it was the City of Jerusalem or not, I cannot say, but I do know that it was a restored city, and everything about it was beautiful.

The Lord finished by saying, 'Embrace Me, Tom, and help them to embrace Me. Pray for them. Build the walls anew, Nehemiah.'"

A couple of weeks after receiving the word from the Lord I recorded at the beginning of this chapter, the Lord once again spoke to me and said, "Tom, I require only two things of you. Seek My face and rebuild my city, Nehemiah." Things are coming full circle. We have crossed the threshold. Interestingly, at the time of this writing, we have once again moved out of the eleventh month (November) – the season of disorder and chaos into the twelfth month (December) – the season of apostolic order. We are in the eighth year following my first revelation of reformation. Eight is the season of new beginnings and new places. Let's finish the work! Let's take our place – even if we are only cupbearers – as gates.

FINISH THE WORK.
Let's turn to Nehemiah 7:1.

Then it was, when the wall was built and I had hung the doors, when the gatekeepers, the singers, and the Levites had been appointed, that I gave the charge of Jerusalem to my brother Hanani, and Hananiah the leader of the citadel, for he was a faithful man and feared God more than many. And I said to them, "Do not let the gates of Jerusalem be opened until the sun is hot; and while they stand guard, let them shut and bar the doors; and appoint guards from among the inhabitants of Jerusalem, one at his watch station and another in front of his own house" (Nehemiah 7:1-3).

The wall is built. The doors of the gates are hung. The gatekeepers, the singers and the Levites have been appointed. As the newly appointed Governor of Jerusalem (Judea), Nehemiah appointed two men to watch over Jerusalem. I believe their names are significant. The first is Hanani. He is Nehemiah's brother. His name means gracious and at the root of the word there is also a meaning which implies favor, prayer and supplication.

God is establishing gatekeepers and guardians of His city who will watch it with prayers, supplications, and intercessions. God's grace and favor will be released over the city. I shared earlier that a transformed city

149

is not necessarily perfect and sinless, but it is a place in which the glory of God is more prevalent than the darkness of Satan. And in some places the darkness is hardly noticeable.

One such place is Almolonga, Guatemala. This city of 20,000 has experienced God's transforming power. Once filled with sin, darkness, alcoholism, depravity, multiple jails and failing crops, its population is now 95% saved and filled with God's Holy Spirit. The jails have all closed. Everyone's businesses are not only named after but they are dedicated to the glory of God. Before transformation only a few trucks would leave the city each month with exported produce. They now have hundreds of trucks leaving and the produce is bigger and richer than any other they've ever seen.

God's grace and favor has touched Almolonga. One of the Pastors of that city is Pastor Mariano Riscajche. His own life is a remarkable and miraculous testimony. He was divinely dropped into our church on December 6, 2006 and He personally, as God's gate, opened up the heavens to be poured out on Prince of Peace Church and all the surrounding region of Dallas and Fort Worth. In November of 2012, I was able to visit his church in Almolonga. We were in Guatemala to visit my youngest daughter, Amy. It was amazing to witness firsthand the ongoing transformation of the city.

I love gates. I love being one of God's gates. His gates release grace, power and favor from His heart into the city.

And that's the name of the second gatekeeper – Hananiah. His name has the identical root of Hanani but it includes the name of God. His name literally means "Yahweh has favored." Yahweh has released His favor and Jerusalem is now rebuilt. Nehemiah's cry of repentance has produced the desired outcome. Yahweh's favor is released on Arlington and on your city. His favor is being released on your state and mine.

## WE ARE POSITIONED!

Nehemiah also gives instructions on watching and guarding the gates. The work of watching is to be done on the walls, the towers and in front of the homes. And it was to be done by the inhabitants of the city. In other words—everyone in the city is positioned as a watcher or gatekeeper. We all have the responsibility of not only being a gate through which the Lord can enter, but also to be a gatekeeper who will watch over and protect the work of His kingdom.

"And He has made from one blood every nation of men to dwell on all the face of the earth, and has determined their preappointed times and the boundaries of their dwellings, so that they should seek the Lord, in the hope that they might grope for Him and find Him, though He is not far from each one of us; for in Him we live and move and have our being, as also some of your own poets have said, 'For we are also His offspring'" (Acts 17:26-28).

Chuck Pierce is his new book, <u>One Thing</u>, said:

"Where we live and why we live there are both part of our abiding and security...We can separate our spiritual abiding place from our physical habitat, but touching God in the midst of the physical habitat is key to our lives being free from anxiety. Acts 17:26 says that He predetermines the place that you're to seek Him. In that predetermined physical place, you will begin to find Him spiritually and gain the strategy necessary to secure your portion."[66]

I'm not sure if this was Chuck's intent but there are times when people disregard or disdain the place where they live and work. They escape the physical place by seeking that spiritual refuge with God and "hang in there" until He finally takes them someplace better or home to heaven. But our true security, identity and purpose will not come until we can meet Him where we live – the place He has determined us to be. Nehemiah could have griped and complained that He was kept as a captive in a foreign land and as a cupbearer of a king who did not honor His God. But He did not. Instead, through prayer, fasting and worship He entered into God's presence in the midst of His physical location and God granted Him the favor, joy and responsibility of being a gate – positioned by God – to be used for the transformation of His city. What could have ended in trauma and curse was released in blessing – the setting forth of God's destiny for a people, a city and a nation.

LET US PRAY

Lord, You have established me in the place of my abiding. Set me into this place as a gatekeeper. Open my eyes to see my assignment as a gate to bring forth Your kingdom into this place. Let me only move at the impulse of Your love and Spirit. I desire to see Your kingdom and will manifested right here! Amen.

# 16

## The Finishing pieces

*"Therefore, with joy you will draw water from the wells of salvation. And in that day, you will say: 'Praise the LORD, call upon His name; declare His deeds among the peoples, make mention that His name is exalted. Sing to the LORD, for He has done excellent things; this is known in all the earth. Cry out and shout, O inhabitant of Zion, for great is the Holy One of Israel in your midst'"*

*(ISAIAH 12:3-6)!*

### THE SETTING FORTH OF A DESTINY

What could have ended in trauma and curse was released in blessing – the setting forth of God's destiny for a people, a city and a nation. What will it look like? I have often been asked by others and I have often asked myself – what will a transformed city look like? What am I longing for? What will be the signs that God's destiny for us has been fulfilled? I believe one significant piece of evidence will be this: the glory and presence of God will be more obviously present than the presence of evil. The city of Almolonga, Guatemala that I referred to in an earlier chapter is another obvious picture of transformation, but let us turn once more to Nehemiah to get some further clues. Read Nehemiah 8:1-6.

Now all the people gathered together as one man in the open square that was in front of the Water Gate; and they told Ezra the scribe to bring the Book of the Law of Moses, which the LORD had commanded Israel. So, Ezra the priest brought the Law before the assembly of men and women and all who could hear with understanding on the first day of the seventh month. Then he read from it in the open square that was in front of the Water Gate from morning until midday, before the men and women and those who could understand; and the ears of all the people were attentive to the Book of the Law. So, Ezra the scribe stood on a platform of wood which they had made for the purpose; and beside him, at his right hand, stood Mattithiah, Shema, Anaiah, Urijah, Hilkiah, and Maaseiah; and at his left hand Pedaiah, Mishael, Malchijah, Hashum, Hashbadana, Zechariah, and Meshullam. And Ezra opened the book in the sight of all the people, for he was standing above all the people; and when he opened it, all the people stood up. And Ezra blessed the LORD, the great God. Then all the people answered, "Amen, Amen!" while lifting up their hands. And they bowed their heads and worshiped the LORD with their faces to the ground.

All the people (not just some) will be gathered as one (not in division but in unity) in the open square (not hidden away in a building but out in the open marketplace), and they will be willing to stand all day for the privilege of hearing (with attentiveness) the Word of God. And their response to the Word will be a time of heartfelt and expressive worship of the Lord God. On Tuesday, December 12, 2006, Chuck Pierce spoke the following words over Arlington, Texas as we were gathered in morning prayers at Glory of Zion Ministries in Denton, Texas: "We release an awakening that will hit Arlington and it will be heard on the news throughout the nation that there is a move of God. We declare that the new stadium will one day be filled with a move of God representing the entire Metroplex. We decree that Arlington has been put on the radar of God and you will be seen."

I do not believe that that bleep on the radar will be a local church having huge crowds at a revival meeting. I do not believe that that signal to the world will be a stadium filled with Christians. I believe that that reading on the radar screen will be a massive shift or transformation of not only a city but of an entire region from the realm of darkness into the realm of

God's kingdom. As I shared in Chapter Two, I believe it will be the day when the city of Arlington and the whole area of Dallas-Fort Worth will stand as one before God as priests. And the subsequent reactions will be the world wanting to drink what we are drinking. Please do not misunderstand my dreams. What happens in this area will not happen here exclusively. It is my earnest prayer that person after person, city after city, and nation after nation will be transformed by God's glory as they seek His face. And it will release a thirst for God into the nations.

## THE FEAST OF TABERNACLES

"Now on the second day the heads of the fathers' houses of all the people, with the priests and Levites, were gathered to Ezra the scribe, in order to understand the words of the Law. And they found written in the Law, which the LORD had commanded by Moses, that the children of Israel should dwell in booths during the feast of the seventh month, and that they should announce and proclaim in all their cities and in Jerusalem, saying, 'Go out to the mountain, and bring olive branches, branches of oil trees, myrtle branches, palm branches, and branches of leafy trees, to make booths, as it is written.' Then the people went out and brought them and made themselves booths, each one on the roof of his house, or in their courtyards or the courts of the house of God, and in the open square of the Water Gate and in the open square of the Gate of Ephraim. So, the whole assembly of those who had returned from the captivity made booths and sat under the booths; for since the days of Joshua the son of Nun until that day the children of Israel had not done so. And there was very great gladness. Also, day by day, from the first day until the last day, he read from the Book of the Law of God. And they kept the feast seven days; and on the eighth day there was a sacred assembly, according to the prescribed manner (Nehemiah 8:13-18).

In these verses of Nehemiah, the people were gathered at the Water Gate in Jerusalem. That same gate was present during the ministry of Jesus and that same gate (possibly a great prophetic act of God's present-day intentions) has been uncovered and excavated in modern Jerusalem. It is the location of the Pool of Siloam. These verses describe the Feast of

Tabernacles. It was a feast that had not been held since the time of Joshua. It occurs five days after the Day of Atonement on the fifteenth of Tishri (October). This feast is also called the Feast of Ingathering (Exodus 23:16; 34:22), the Feast to the Lord (Leviticus 23:39; Judges 21:9), the Feast of Booths, or simply "the feast" (Leviticus 23:36; Deuteronomy 16:13; I Kings 8:2; II Chronicles 5:3, 7:8; Nehemiah 8:14; Isaiah 30:29; Ezekiel 45:23,25). The people are instructed to go and collect "olive branches, branches of oil trees, myrtle branches, palm branches, and branches of leafy trees" in order to build their booths.

"On the first day of the feast, each participant had to collect twigs of myrtle, willow, and palm in the area of Jerusalem for construction of their booth (Nehemiah 8:13-18). These "huts" or "booths" were constructed from bulrushes as joyful reminders of the temporary housing erected by their forefathers during the Exodus wanderings (Leviticus 23:40-41; Deuteronomy 16:14). The "booth" in Scripture is a symbol of protection, preservation, and shelter from heat and storm (Psalm 27:5; 31:20; Isaiah 4:6). The rejoicing community included family, servants, orphans, widows, Levites, and sojourners (Deuteronomy 16:13-15)."[67]

On the eighth and final day of the feast, the high priest of Israel, in a great processional made up of priests and tens of thousands of worshipers, descended from the Temple Mount to pause briefly at the Pool of Siloam. A golden pitcher was filled with water, and the procession continued back to the Temple. The high priest poured the water out of the pitcher onto the altar. During the procession, the people recited Isaiah 12:3-6:

Therefore, with joy you will draw water from the wells of salvation. And in that day, you will say: "Praise the LORD, call upon His name; declare His deeds among the peoples, make mention that His name is exalted. Sing to the LORD, for He has done excellent things; this is known in all the earth. Cry out and shout, O inhabitant of Zion, for great is the Holy One of Israel in your midst!"

Salvation will spring forth. All the peoples will declare His praise! The nations will exalt the name of the Lord. He will be known in all the earth! These are signs of transformation, restoration and healing.

It was also at the Feast of Tabernacles and on this eighth day that the gospel of John records a fascinating event. John wrote: "In the last day (eighth day), that great day of the feast, Jesus stood and cried out, saying, If any man thirst, let him come unto me, and drink. He that believeth on me, as the scripture hath said, out of his heart shall flow rivers of living water" (John 7:37-38). The Son of God was saying in the clearest possible way that He alone was the source of life, healing and blessing; that He and only He could meet every need of the human heart. Only He can transform a whole city and region so that it shows up on world radar.

Jesus is calling to anyone who thirsts to come to Him. He is the One and the only One who turns our weeping into joy. He turns our lamenting into thanksgiving. He turns our sorrow into praise. He turns death into life. When He enters into a person or a city as the King of Glory, He turns chaos and darkness into order and light. He invites all of us to drink of Him. "Tabernacles speaks of the day when the Son of God will tabernacle among men, wipe away every tear, and bring in the 'golden age' which men have dreamed of since time immemorial."[68]

## WE MUST REMEMBER!

Jerusalem is celebrating. The feast is a declaration of the salvation and provision of God. In the last chapters of Nehemiah, the covenant of God's promised relationship with His people will be read and renewed, the walls will be dedicated and the life of the city and its inhabitants will be brought into divine order. The city is restored. God wants the whole city to come to Him as priests – seeking His intimacy and moving with His authority.

We must remember where this all began. It started within the palace walls at Susa. It started with an enslaved servant, a cupbearer, who responded with a Holy Spirit-initiated confession of sins. **It started with one person who had a heart willing to be used by God as a gate.** Nehemiah was willing and eager for the Lord to move through Him to bring about, in an almost impossible scenario, the restoration of an entire city and nation.

## WHAT CAN WE DO?

As we head into these closing paragraphs I am not as interested in giving you detailed or technical instructions about "taking your city." There are many excellent books dedicated to that topic. Instead I want to draw us back to the simplicity of Nehemiah's call. It was simple yet profound. It was small yet it had earthshaking ramifications.

**Seek the Lord.** Nehemiah's heart was turned toward God. It all begins and ends with us seeking His face. There is absolutely nothing more essential than God's call for each of us to come into His presence and to know Him. The birth of all transformation happens when our hearts are bound up in the Father's heart and His thoughts and desires become our thoughts and desires. Let your life be dictated and determined by the time you spend with Him in extravagant worship, praise and prayer. Let everything you do be an expression of worship. Yesterday (January 9, 2007), I joined ten other pastors and leaders from the Tarrant County area in prayer. Arlington and Fort Worth are both major cities in Tarrant County. This revelation of seeking the Lord fell on us corporately as we gathered for prayer. We proclaimed our desire to passionately seek the face of the Lord. We proclaimed and covenanted our desire to adjust our heavy and hectic schedules to dedicate a time to come together weekly for prayer and worship. The Spirit of the Lord fell on us. I prophesied during the meeting: "The Lord says, 'Set the time! Set the day! It's make no difference. I have heard your cries and I will meet with you. Set the time! Set the day! I will come into your midst.'" Amen and amen. God promises to meet with those who draw near to Him.

**Acknowledge who you are in Him.** Nehemiah was in exile. He had not yet returned to Jerusalem. He was a cupbearer of the king – valuable but expendable. Most importantly he recognized that he was a servant of the Lord God Almighty. You are a redeemed child of the King. You might be a student, a teacher, a plumber, a corporate executive, a pastor, a nurse, an adult, a child or a cupbearer, but ultimately you are a person positioned by God as a **gate** in order to allow the glory, majesty, holiness, righteousness, life, light and blessing of God to go through you and to penetrate the world in which you live.

We no longer have the privilege or right to say "I think someone else is better suited for this. I don't qualify. I don't have the right knowledge, position or experience." Any person, regardless of their race, age, sex or vocation, which passionately seeks the Lord and acknowledges that they belong to Him will be used by God to bring forth His kingdom in this hour. Declare now as you read this: "Here I am Lord, use me."

**Confess.** With his heart tuned into God's heart, Nehemiah was quick to repent when he discovered the condition of his people and his city. We are in a time of visitation. God is moving among us. As I shared at the beginning of Chapter 14 God has placed us in a new place and He has started His reforming and transforming work. It is now time to present ourselves as clean vessels before Him. We must not tarry or delay in our actions. Nehemiah quickly responded. As we invite the King of Glory into our city, we need to be gates with no obstructions.

Ask the Lord to cleanse your life. Ask the Lord to examine every thought, relationship, intention, dream and plan – even those that you received from Him. It is important that we are stepping into His plans and purposes and not asking Him to come and bless ours. Several weeks ago, the Lord awakened me and told me to examine every relationship in my life. As I literally brought each relationship before Him beginning with my family and including all my ministry connections, He gave me specific instructions regarding each of them.

Ask the Lord to reveal to you the sins you have committed. Remember that the Greek word for sin (hamartia) is translated as sin but the root word (hamartano) means "to miss the mark (and so not share in the prize)."[69] Lord, when or where have I missed the mark? What thoughts or acts have I committed which are out of alignment with You and Your plans for my life, my family, my work, my ministry, my city, etc.? I shared with the other leaders I met with yesterday that I did not want to miss out of God's visitation. I do not want to miss the mark. I do not want to miss out on the prize. Therefore, it is essential that I allow Him to thoroughly examine my life.

And not only do we confess our own "missed marks" but also the sins committed by past generations which are standing in the way of God's transforming power. Be quick to repent. Seek the forgiving and healing hand of God to come upon you and your city.

**Act.** Nehemiah acted. His first action was repentance. His second action was fasting and prayer. Let me say that again. His first action was repentance. His second action was fasting and prayer. His third action was directly tied to the first two and happened as a divinely appointed act by God. He responded to the divine-prompted question of King Artaxerxes. As a pastor, I am in fellowship with many other church leaders in the city, state and nation. In most of those places of fellowship there is a "buzz" of activity as men and women are trying to discover the next action, the next plan, or the next formula that will carry them into the next level of God's kingdom. I can remember sitting among pastors in the City of Arlington – who had come together to pray – sharing their newest idea for outreach, church growth, missions, city-reaching, etc. And yet we never prayed. When we announce a new unified effort of outreach that is going to "change the city" many are on board. When we announce that we are gathering for prayer and waiting for God to meet with us and direct us – few sign up for the cause. Do not misunderstand me. God wants us to act as His servants, lights, priests, and warriors **but we must act in obedience** to His words spoken out of **the womb of prayer** and worship and not out of our own zeal to do the right thing.

Let me give you an example. There was Native American massacre that took place in San Antonio in 1840. The Lord started revealing the details of this massacre to me during a time of prayer and worship during another reconciliation event in which I was participating near Amarillo, Texas. The Lord led me to a book and then to other books and articles. I just keep praying for understanding and wisdom. He has subsequently told me that this event is a key issue in unlocking doors of forgiveness and healing into the State of Texas. I knew from my prayers and reading who the key participants for reconciliation needed to be. It was going to require the participation of the Governor's office, the Comanche Nation, a member of the military and key church leaders from around the state. I knew some of the people to contact but most of the participants were outside my realm of relationship, influence or authority. I kept praying.

The first week of January 2007 (eight months after first hearing about the massacre) while I was attending the "Starting the Year Off Right" conference led by Chuck Pierce and Glory of Zion International in Denton, Texas the Lord brought everything to a head. During a time of worship and prophetic declaration the Lord "out of the blue" divinely connected me with two representatives of the Comanche Nation and within the next twelve hours connected me with key Texas leaders and an open door to the Governor's office. I know that this reconciliation will take place in the next few weeks – not because I forced it to happen – but because God wants it to happen and I have given myself to Him as a prayerful and obedient participant. When I shared this action with another prayer leader in the state she informed that she has been praying for years that God would deal with this issue.

We must wait on Him. We must seek His face. We must line ourselves up with God in worship, prayer and fasting. And when He provides the opportunity we must obediently take action.

## IN CLOSING

The Lord God of heaven and earth loves us. He wants us to come into the fullness of our destiny as His children. He wants to touch our lives with His grace, love and power so that we will touch others. He wants to release heaven on earth. He wants His will to be done in our midst. He wants to transform our cities from places of darkness into places filled with His light and glory. He wants to enter into our world as King and Lord of all. He needs gates to come through. He needs you and me. Lift up your heads O gates and let the King of Glory come in! And He will come in and He will restore!

For thus says the LORD: After seventy years are completed at Babylon, I will visit you and perform My good word toward you, and cause you to return to this place. For I know the thoughts that I think toward you, says the LORD, thoughts of peace and not of evil, to give you a future and a hope. Then you will call upon Me and go and pray to Me, and I will listen to you. **And you will seek Me and find Me, when you search for Me with all your heart. I will be found by you, says the LORD, and I will**

**bring you back from your captivity;** I will gather you from all the nations and from all the places where I have driven you, says the LORD, and I will bring you to the place from which I cause you to be carried away captive. (Jeremiah 29:10-14, **emphasis mine**).

# 17

## It's 2017

*"I kept looking, and that horn was waging war with the saints and overpowering them until the Ancient of Days came and judgment was passed in favor of the saints of the Highest One, and the time arrived when the saints took possession of the kingdom"*

(DANIEL *7:21-22*).

just returned from Washington D.C. as I am putting the last touches on this manuscript for the 2017 Edition. We were on an assignment which called for the opening up of new gates of righteousness into the city and nation. In just a week from now (July 27, 2017), it will be the 4th of Av. That is the date on the Jewish calendar when the work on the
Jerusalem walls will begin under Nehemiah. The Lord reminded me on the trip that the first gate restored was the Sheep Gate by the High Priest Eliashib. The Sheep Gate is important since the sheep used for sacrifices would be brought through this gate into the city. You will remember that the Priest Eliashib was the one who had allowed the enemy (Tobiah the Ammonite) into the temple (Nehemiah 13:1-9). We declare, as we build

up and open up this new gate that Tobiah must vacate the premises. He can no longer have access. Remember that keys represent access. We hold the keys.

He also brought to my attention Daniel 7:21-22 which declares: "I kept looking, and that horn was waging war with the saints and overpowering them until the Ancient of Days came and judgment was passed in favor of the saints of the Highest One, and the time arrived when the saints took possession of the kingdom."

Now is that time! The gates need rebuilding. The walls need to rise up from the rubble. We need to use the apostolic authority that the Lord has granted us to open these gates with the keys with which we are entrusted. A new sheep gate of redemption is released into the possession of the saints. We declare "your kingdom come and Your will be done" over Texas, Washington D.C., Israel and the nations of the earth.

## BRADDOCK'S ROCK -- THE KEY OF KEYS

As you drive up the entrance ramp to the Theodore Roosevelt bridge from Constitution Avenue in Washington D.C., you'll pass by a stone well with an iron cover. This is a remnant of an old Washington landmark known as Braddock's Rock, the Key of Keys. This is where General Braddock landed on his way to Fort Duquesne, in 1755. The rock is no longer at the water's edge. The filling in of the bay and the Tidal Basin has placed a thousand feet of land between the Key of Keys and the present bank of the Potomac.

Significantly, this rock was a "key" to Washington, as it was used as the beginning survey point by which all of the city was laid out. The rock was eventually blasted and quarried to be used for construction. Large quantities of the stone were used in the construction of public buildings, such as the foundations of the Capitol and the White House.

To say the least, for a person whose last name means "Keeper of the Keys," this is an important landmark for our nation's capital. As I have done before, I declare the following from the spiritual Key of Keys (the Key of David) that has been granted to us:

## OPEN THE GATES

"Lift up your heads, O you gates!
And be lifted up, you everlasting doors!
And the King of glory shall come in.
Who is this King of glory?
The LORD strong and mighty,
The LORD mighty in battle.
Lift up your heads, O you gates!
Lift up, you everlasting doors!
And the King of glory shall come in.
Who is this King of glory?
The LORD of hosts,
He is the King of glory" (Psalm 24:7-10).

Rejoice in the Lord! It is the day of new beginnings. The gates are open.
I decree as a keeper of keys that the gates are open to the King of Glory.

I decree the opening of the gates of minds and hearts to the kingdom of
our God.
I decree the opening of our minds and hearts to the wisdom and revela-
tion of our Lord Jesus Christ.
Be opened to the Spirit of the living God – the Holy One.
Be opened to salvation, life, hope, peace and joy in the Holy Spirit.
Let the waves of the Lord's love and mercy be released into each of us.

I decree the opening of our homes and businesses to the King of
Glory.
I decree the opening of the gates of our cities to the King of
Righteousness.
Join me in flinging wide the gates of Arlington, Texas or **wherever** you
live.
We invite the Lord of hosts!

We invite the fullness of His kingdom and His will to be manifested in our midst.

I decree the opening of the gates of Texas.
I remind the Lord of the places where we stood before Him and welcomed Him.
I decree the shores of the Gulf Coast open.
I decree the mountains of West Texas open.
I decree the sprawling lands of the Valley and the high plains of the Panhandle open.
I decree the Piney Woods and the Rolling Plains open.
I decree the farmlands of central Texas and the Hill Country open.
I decree the rivers open to the King of Glory.
I decree the cities and towns to be open to the King.
I decree the government, the educational systems, the families, the media, the arts and entertainment arenas, the businesses and the churches of Texas open to
the Lord God Almighty – the everlasting One.
I take the keys of the kingdom and open Texas and our surrounding covenant States
to the presence of King Jesus.
His kingdom come, His will be done on earth as it is in heaven.
I decree the blowing of His wind across the land.
I decree the river of God to rise.
I decree the floodgates of heaven to open.
I decree the structures opposed to the Kingdom of God to crumble and fall in the name of Jesus!

On this day, I cry to the Lord of heaven and earth and
decree open the gates of Washington DC and the United States.
Let the gates of righteousness and of God's kingdom be opened in the Spirit.
Flood the land, O Lord, with Your presence.
The King of Glory shall come in!

# Epilogue

*"Behold, I stand at the door and knock. If anyone hears My voice and opens the door, I will come in to him and dine with him, and he with Me"*

(REVELATION 3:20).

## HABITATION NOT VISITATION

In Chapter Fifteen I shared how I had participated in a passionate time of prayer with ten other Christian leaders from Tarrant County. During the end of the meeting I declared to them, "I do not want God to visit us. I want Him to be enthroned in our midst. I want Him to take up habitation with us."

Chuck Pierce in his book <u>Reordering Your Day: Understanding and Embracing the Four Prayer Watches</u> writes: "Revival is not found by urging repentance (even though God wants us to repent). It does not result from seeking unity (although unity is important). It does not come by seeking harvest. It is not achieved by seeking city transformation. In fact, REVIVAL IS NOT FOUND BY SEEKING REVIVAL. Revival comes – God's presence comes – when we seek HIM with all our hearts!"[70]

The classic definition of revival is a time of the Lord's visitation. The Lord visits us and we are changed, renewed, saved, transformed and healed. Yes, and amen! I long for Him to visit us. But I have passionately longed for something more. I want Him to be enthroned in our midst. The prophet Jeremiah declared: "O the Hope of Israel, his Savior in time of trouble, why should You be like a stranger in the land, and like a traveler who turns aside to tarry for a night? Why should You be like a man astonished, like a mighty one who cannot save? Yet You, O LORD, are in our midst, and we are called by Your name; do not leave us" (Jeremiah 14:8-9)!

I do not want the Lord to tarry with us just a day or night. I want Him to be found in our midst. I want Him to be established as a habitation in the midst of His people. I want Him enthroned in our city. I want the city walls restored. I want the gates to be in place and swung open to greet Him. I want the lives of all the people to be changed. I want Him to dwell in our midst. The verb "to dwell" in the Hebrew is "shakan." Shakan is the root to the Hebrew word Shekinah. Shekinah is the manifested or revealed glory or presence of God. God promised His people Israel at Mt. Sinai that if they built a sanctuary for Him that He would come and dwell (shakan) in their midst. He will dwell in their midst with His glorious presence. We were told that the "Word became flesh and dwelt among us, and we beheld His glory, the glory as of the only begotten of the Father, full of grace and truth" (John 1:14).

God desires to enthrone Himself in our midst and He does just that when we seek Him and Him alone. When we lift our heart, voices and hands in praise and worship (not only individually but corporately) He enthrones Himself in our midst (Psalm 22:3). Out of God's presence, all the signs of revival and transformation will flow.

"His LIFE is a magnet to draw the lost. People are attracted to LIFE. In stories of revival, people show up in church without even knowing why they have come. They have responded to an inner urge they cannot explain. There is something about the presence of God that draws people to Him. His HOLINESS moves sinful believers to repentance. A lot of times we try to persuade people to repent. When the presence of God comes, persuasion is not usually necessary. When God shows up, people repent because they see the reality of His holiness. His POWER brings healing, miracles and faith for answered prayer. When God manifests His presence, it is not hard to see miracles. Miracles are we He naturally does!"[71]

If this is your desire as well, then rise up Nehemiah! Seek the face of the Lord. Passionately pursue Him in prayer and worship. Rebuild the walls. Set the gates in place. Swing them wide open and declare – King of Glory – come in! I decree to you that God is faithful. He will come as a response to our cries! Seek out fellowship among the saints. Reach across every man-made barrier for the hand of God and see the barriers fall. The Lord is looking for a place to dwell. Why not among us?

The Lord continues to open up my life to new gates. In June of 2007 Chuck Pierce commissioned me as the new coordinator of the newly formed Texas Apostolic Prayer Network. The Lord met with us in Austin, Texas. Shortly thereafter, Dr. John Benefiel, Dutch Sheets, Jay Swallow, Negiel Bigpond, Sandy Newman from Kansas and others commissioned me as an Apostle out of the Heartland Apostolic Prayer Network.

It demonstrates two things. First – that God can take a cupbearer from a small congregation tucked away in East Arlington and use him to bring about shifts at a statewide and nationwide level. And second – get ready all you cupbearers to be used by God.

## WE ARE KEEPERS OF THE KEYS

We are keepers of the keys. We are gates. Press on to victory. Let your hair down and take the lead. It is a new day. We have new strategies, weapons and winds. God demonstrated His response to the meeting in Austin as 80 miles per hour winds blew through the heart of Texas within an hour after the meeting. A lightning show, beyond all others, was displayed in the skies. Our God reigns over Texas. Our God reigns over the nation. Our God reigns over the nations. It's a Nehemiah season and we are on the road to reformation and transformation.

# Appendix One

## BIRD'S FORT

In 1835 Caddo lands in Louisiana were ceded by treaty between the Caddo and the United States. The treaty required the Caddo to leave the boundaries of the United States within a year. They headed to the northern regions of Texas. In 1836, following the War of Independence with Mexico, there were increasing tensions between Native Americans located in North Texas and the increasing population of Anglos migrating from the United States. Great attempts were made by the President of the Republic of Texas, Sam Houston, to make peace with the Native American Nations, but hostilities were still present. Hostilities escalated when Mirabeau B. Lamar became the second President of Texas. His goal was to rid Texas of all Native Americans.

On May 24, 1841, a small militia of seventy led by General Tarrant journeyed to the region around the Trinity River and Village Creek area to deal with the tribes that had been raiding North Texas homes. Though populated by over a thousand persons in an accumulation of several Indian Nations (Caddo, Waco, Anadarko, Cherokee, Kickapoos and others), most of the warriors were off hunting. General Tarrant attacked the Village Creek area and killed many (mostly women, children and elderly). Captain John Denton was the only Anglo killed. In July of the same year a larger militia force of four hundred returned to the area and found it deserted. The Tribes had moved west of the Brazos River. The empty villages along Village Creek were burned.

In late summer of 1841 Bird's Fort was built just north of the Trinity River in present day Arlington to provide an Anglo presence and protection in the area. In November of 1841 John Neely Bryan came back to Texas via Bird's Fort. He had first visited the area in 1839. He traveled down river and settled on the east bank of the Trinity River, not far from the present location of downtown Dallas. In the spring of 1842 he persuaded several families who had settled at Bird's Fort to join him. On September 29, 1943 negotiations began at the fort between Republic of Texas officials (Gen. Tarrant and Gen. George W. Terrell) and the leaders of nine Indian tribes. The meetings ended on September 29, 1843, with the signing of the Bird's Fort Treaty. Terms of the agreement called for an end to existing conflicts and the establishment of a line separating Indian lands from territory open for colonization. The terms included the understanding that from the forks of the Trinity on a line to the southwest to Menard, the western side would be red man's hunting ground, while the east would be the white man's farm land. Beyond the border was "Where the West Begins." Only authorized delegations, such as teachers, blacksmiths and licensed traders, could cross into Indian Territory. Trading posts would be built along the line. Property belonging to one side found on the other side would be restored to its proper owner through post offi-cials. These ceremonies were the high point in the history of the fort. But not long after the ceremonies, the fort was considered uninhabitable. A band of Indians burned the grass around the fort causing a lack of game and forage. Though it was reoccupied time and again, the winters and the Indians always proved too severe and more than a few lives were lost.

In 1846 Captain Middleton Tate Johnson built a trading station to the south. Often referred to as Johnson's Station, it succeeded where Bird's Fort had not, providing pioneers with "end of the trail" necessities to settle their new homes. Johnson's Station would later become part of Arlington. On June 6, 1849 Johnson and Brevet Major Ripley A. Arnold established a fort and army outpost at the junction of the Clear Fork and the West Fork of the Trinity River. They named it Fort Worth in honor of Gen. William J. Worth. Johnson also helped to organize Tarrant County. Between the years of 1843-1859 the line between Native Americans and Anglos, after more dispute, hostilities and broken promises, became wider and the Natives were eventually pushed out of the area.

# About the Author

Thomas Schlueter has been Pastor of Prince of Peace House of Prayer, a strategic house of prayer in Arlington Texas, for 29 years. Pastor Schlueter obtained a Bachelor's degree at Texas A&M University before receiving his Masters of Divinity at Wartburg Theological Seminary. He received his Doctor of Ministry in July 2006 from Christian Leadership University in New York.

Pastor Schlueter's ministry extends beyond Prince of Peace House of Prayer and the Dallas-Fort Worth region. He is the Founder of Arlington Prayer Net, a network of prayer leaders from churches and ministries in Arlington and surrounding communities. The purpose of the network is to come alongside the pastoral staffs of local churches to start, strengthen and expand prayer ministries in the church.

He has also been appointed as the Apostolic Coordinator of the Texas Apostolic Prayer Network, which desires to see the redemptive anointing of the State to flow freely. They desire the people, the history, the culture, and the destiny of Texas to be transformed as the Lord is enthroned in our midst.

He serves as the Texas and South Central United States Regional Leader of the Heartland Apostolic Prayer Network directed by Apostle John Benefiel of Church on the Rock of Oklahoma City. He also serves as the Texas and South Central United States Regional Leader of the Reformation Prayer Network directed by Apostles Cindy and Mike Jacobs of Generals International. Pastor Schlueter teaches prayer and Bible seminars locally and internationally. Pastor Schlueter is in covenant relationship with Dr. Chuck Pierce of Global Spheres International and Antioch Oasis International, led by Apostle Olen Griffing.

Pastor Schlueter is actively involved with praying strategically for city government and workplace ministry. He has a passion to see the whole city of Arlington, Texas, the State of Texas and the heartland regions of the United States come into their full redemptive purpose. He also has a zeal for developing a strong covenant relationship with the First Nations people. He desires to witness the releasing of the full destiny of God into their lives as the first peoples of our nation.

He is the author of <u>Return of the Priests</u>, a book declaring that God is restoring a kingdom of priests in our generation-not a priesthood defined by clerical collars and religious rituals. Rather it is a priesthood of everyday people walking intimately with God, who act and speak with life-changing authority in their homes, neighborhoods, and workplaces.

He is married to Kay Sanders Schlueter, and they have three grown children: Josh and his wife Andrea, Katie and her husband Tim, and Amy and her husband Allan. The couple has four grandchildren.

**Contact:**
Thomas Schlueter Prince of Peace House of Prayer
Texas Apostolic Prayer Network
1712 Herschel Street
Arlington, Texas 76010
pt4texas@gmail.com

# Endnotes

1. Thomas Schlueter, *Return of the Priests* (Arlington, Texas: Prince of Peace Press, 2004), p. 22, 23.

2. http://www.lightthehighway.org/en/index.php/Main_Page

3. Sam Brassfield, Spring 2007 at Heartland World Ministries Church in Las Colinas, Texas.

4. Kevin J. Conner, Interpreting the Symbols and Types (Portland, Oregon: City Bible Publishing, 1980), p. 54.

5. Ibid., p.54

6. This is a paraphrase of a message given by George Otis, Jr. on September 18, 2007 in Dallas.

7. Ibid., p.55

8. Intercessors International is now called Increase International. It is still overseen by its founders – Beth and Floyd Alves.

9. This quote was taken from my personal notes at the 2004 Board Meeting of Intercessors International in Arlington, Texas.

10. In my book Return of the Priests I commented on Dutch's declaration that I recorded at a Washington D.C. meeting. The Lord is moving us from priestly intercession only into a kingly or governmental intercession. The Lord has moved Dutch into this realm as he has decreed and declared God's purposes throughout our nation but especially in Washington D.C.

11. Dutch Sheets, Authority in Prayer (Bloomington, Minnesota: Bethany House Publishers, 2006), p. 121.

12. Thomas Schlueter, Return of the Priests (Arlington, Texas: Prince of Peace Press, 2002004), p.179.

13. Ibid, p. 179-80.

14. Videos and other products by George Otis, Jr. can be ordered at http://www.sentinelgroup.org/

15. This journey from a soul-driven life to one driven by the Spirit of God is dealt masterfully in Dutch Sheet's new book, Roll Away Your Stone.

16. Biblesoft's New Exhaustive Strong's Numbers and Concordance with Expanded Greek-Hebrew Dictionary. Copyright (c) 1994, Biblesoft and International Bible Translators, Inc.

17. Biblesoft's New Exhaustive Strong's Numbers and Concordance with Expanded Greek-Hebrew Dictionary. Copyright (c) 1994, Biblesoft and International Bible Translators, Inc.

18. On November 5, 2006, I stood as a representative from the State of Texas before Apostle Jay Swallow, Roaming Buffalo of the Cheyenne Nation, and repented for the atrocities and sins that Texas had committed against His nation as well as all other First Nations. His words of forgiveness broke down old walls of bitterness, resentment, sin, trauma and death that had hung over all of us.

19. Based on Exodus 32:7-10.

20. The Message

21. Longfellow, Henry Wadsworth, The Midnight Ride of Paul Revere, viewed 13 September 2006, at www.nationalcenter.org/PaulRevere's Ride.html.

22. This independence is witnessed often among intercessors. Jeanine Smith, our Minister of Prayer stated to me, "I am thinking of the intercessors who have been telling me they don't have to have covering or permission to do whatever they feel God has told them to do because they have 'all authority.' There was lady who attended our church for a while and then moved to another state. She called me about some things she had discovered within a couple of weeks of getting there – places where she sensed darkness, homosexuality etc. She was thinking of going with another lady who had also recently moved there to pull down the strongholds. I suggested that she and the lady get the blessing of their pastor. Neither had found a covering pastor or church yet. I suggested that they wait until they did and consider the authority of the owner of the place. She called me later and said the lady said they didn't need anybody else's permission because they had 'all authority' in Christ and God had told them to do it." This type of independent thinking is dangerous.

23. Kevin J. Conner, Interpreting the Symbols and Types (Portland, Oregon: City Bible Publishing, 1980), p. 53.

24. Thomas Schlueter, Return of the Priests (Arlington, Texas: Prince of Peace Press, 2004), p.61.

25. (Biblesoft's New Exhaustive Strong's Numbers and Concordance with Expanded Greek-Hebrew Dictionary. Copyright (c) 1994, Biblesoft and International Bible Translators, Inc.)

26. Ibid

27. Ibid

28. Nelson's Illustrated Bible Dictionary, Copyright (c)1986, Thomas Nelson Publishers, p.?

29. The Wycliffe Bible Commentary, Electronic Database. Copyright (c) 1962 by Moody Press Check form.

30. More information on "The Anubis Caves" can be read in Chapter 4 of the article "In Plain Sight" by Gloria Farley. The article can be read at http://www2.privatei.com/~bartjean/mainpage.htm.

31. Paul Keith Davis. Thrones of Our Soul (Lake Mary, Florida: Creation House Press, 2003), p. 77, 78).

32. Dr. Ronald E. Cottle, Studies in Nehemiah (Columbus, Georgia: Christian Life Publications, 1997), p. 65.

33. Ibid., p. 103

34. Biblesoft's New Exhaustive Strong's Numbers and Concordance with Expanded Greek-Hebrew Dictionary. Copyright (c) 1994, Biblesoft and International Bible Translators, Inc.

35. Ibid.

36. Dr. Ronald E. Cottle, Studies in Nehemiah (Columbus, Georgia: Christian Life Publications, 1997), p. 63.

37. Thomas Schlueter, Return of the Priests (Arlington, Texas: Prince of Peace Press, 2004), p. 46.

38. Dr. Ronald E. Cottle, Studies in Nehemiah (Columbus, Georgia: Christian Life Publications, 1997), p. 65.

39. Biblesoft's New Exhaustive Strong's Numbers and Concordance with Expanded Greek-Hebrew Dictionary. Copyright (c) 1994, Biblesoft and International Bible Translators, Inc.

40. Biblesoft's New Exhaustive Strong's Numbers and Concordance with Expanded Greek-Hebrew Dictionary. Copyright (c) 1994, Biblesoft and International Bible Translators, Inc.

41. Spiros Zodhiates, ed, Greek-Hebrew Key Word Study Bible (LaHabra, CA: AMG International, Inc. and Lockman Foundation, 1990) p. 1787.

42. Taken from my personal journal during the January 2005 trip to Papua New Guinea and China.

43. Taken from my personal notes at the "City-Wide Prayer Conference" held September 29, 2006 at Gateway Church in Southlake, Texas.

44. Bill Johnson, The Supernatural Power of a Transformed Mind (Shippensburg, PA: Destiny Image Publishers, Inc., 2005), p. 60.

45. Ibid. p. 42.

46. Biblesoft's New Exhaustive Strong's Numbers and Concordance with Expanded Greek-Hebrew Dictionary. Copyright (c) 1994, Biblesoft and International Bible Translators, Inc.

47. Http://en.wikipedia.org/wiki/Pan (mythology).

48. Jack Hayford, Prayer is Invading the Impossible (Gainesville, Florida: Bridge-Logos, 1977), p. 169.

49. Ibid., p. 172.

50. Spiros Zodhiates, ed, Greek-Hebrew Key Word Study Bible (LaHabra, CA: AMG International, Inc. and Lockman Foundation, 1990) p. 1820.

51. Ibid., p. 1820.

52. Jack Hayford, Prayer is Invading the Impossible (Gainesville, Florida: Bridge-Logos, 1977), p. 178.

53. Biblesoft's New Exhaustive Strong's Numbers and Concordance with Expanded Greek-Hebrew Dictionary. Copyright (c) 1994, Biblesoft and International Bible Translators, Inc.

54. Prayer Newsletter from Dutch Sheets, March 2, 2007

55. Biblesoft's New Exhaustive Strong's Numbers and Concordance with Expanded Greek-Hebrew Dictionary. Copyright (c) 1994, Biblesoft and International Bible Translators, Inc.

56. Biblesoft's New Exhaustive Strong's Numbers and Concordance with Expanded Greek-Hebrew Dictionary. Copyright (c) 1994, Biblesoft and International Bible Translators, Inc.

57. The Decree of Divorce that we used was written by Dr. Jerry Mash, a lawyer, who works with Dr. John Benefiel in the Oklahoma Apostolic Prayer Network. This decree has been used in Oklahoma, Texas, Kansas, Missouri and Arkansas. It was produced in response to a prophetic call given by Dutch Sheets at "Starting the Year Off Right" in January 2007 in Denton, Texas. The heartland regions of Texas, Oklahoma, Arkansas and Kansas have flourished under the blessing of God. Drought was broken. Revival is being released. The battle with Baal is not over but the battle is being fought!

58. As I mentioned in a previous chapter, nature itself under the authority of God, not Baal, responded with rain in abundance. A several year

drought ended as lakes that were fifteen to seventeen feet down over-flowed only weeks later. Meteorologists had declared that it would take years to restore the lake levels.

59. Beverly McIntyre, Change Point founder invites you to learn more about Change Point Incorporated, a non-profit organization committed to charting a course for change by meeting the real needs of people at point where there is opposition or depression through reaching out with medical, physical, emotional, and spiritual support. The ministry is located in Arizona and Texas. Information regarding the ministry can be located at www.changepointinc.org/home.

60. John and Lisa Bevere founded Messenger International in 1995. The ministry desires to communicate to the world with life-transforming messages. Information regarding the ministry can be located at www. messengerintl.org.

61. Barbara Yoder, Breaker Anointing

62. Barbara Yoder, Breaker Anointing

63. In September 2007 at a conference at Glory of Zion in Denton, Dutch Sheets had just exhorted us to receive the Jehu or Finishing Anointing. He told us that the backbone of Baal was broken but we must now go to the high places to finish the task. Kay and I, must to our chagrin, had to leave early from the conference. We had an appointment (that had already been changed twice) to visit Beverly and Bobby McIntyre at their new home. When we arrive, we discovered that their home which sat alone on a hill was located at one of the high places in Texas. God had sent us on assignment.

64. My wife Kay and I just spent a weekend with Bobby and Beverly. Their home is located on the highest point in that whole region of Texas. We spent an afternoon praying and decreeing that this high place – now

occupied by the McIntyre's – was literally in the hands of our God and His kingdom. We declared that it no longer was a high place for the enemy.

65. Proverbs 29:18

66. Dr. Chuck D. and Pamela J. Pierce, <u>One Thing</u>, p. 103.

67. http://www.christcenteredmall.com/teachings/feasts/tabernacles.htm

68. Ibid

69. Biblesoft's New Exhaustive Strong's Numbers and Concordance with Expanded Greek-Hebrew Dictionary. Copyright (c) 1994, Biblesoft and International Bible Translators, Inc.

70. Chuck Pierce, Reordering Your Day: Understanding and Embracing the Four Prayer Watches (Denton, Texas: Glory of Zion International Ministries, 2006), p. 90.

71. Ibid, p. 88.

79514858R00119

Made in the USA
Lexington, KY
23 January 2018